The Canal du Midi

– an introduction

By the same author:

Caesar's Passage

"Compellingly realistic, a novel full of suspense and action"

The Canal du Midi

– an introduction

Andrew Smyth

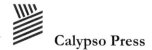

Calypso Press

Published by Calypso Press 2003
15, Camden Square
London NW1 9UY

Published in Britain in 2003

A CIP catalogue record for this book is available from the British Library

ISBN 0-9542270-1-8

With deepest gratitude to my wife, Corinne Julius, not simply for many of the photographs (including the cover) but for so very much more.

Chapters

Introduction

If you're trying to get to the Mediterranean from northern Europe, the most cursory glance at a map of whatever projection shows that the Iberian peninsula is a real nuisance.

A slightly more detailed look would suggest that if you could cut through that narrowing piece of land in South West France at the base of the peninsula, it could save nearly 1,000 nautical miles at sea – as well as an open crossing of the Bay of Biscay, possibly in the gales of winter. If going north, it could avoid fighting against the Portugese trade winds in the summer.

Such a passage not only exists, but has been there for over 300 years. The Canal des Deux Mers, to give it its full title, offers a back-door short cut into the Mediterranean, as well as a unique opportunity to experience a completely different type of cruising. So why don't more people take advantage of it?

There are few more prolific sources of gratuitous advice than people on boats – be it where to moor; how to moor; what you should be doing; what you should have done. For some reason, this advice is even more freely available on the French canals, although when it concerns the Canal du Midi, nearly all of it seems to be negative. An authoritative source at the Cruising Association told me that the Canal "is rarely quoted as a suitable route to or from the Med". And once an area or a passage has developed a certain reputation, it takes a long time to shake it off. Thirteen years after its war with Serbia, people still ask whether Croatia is safe.

Someone who had never been near the canal reported authoritatively that the lock-keepers on the Canal du Midi are well known to be surly and rude. Someone else assured me, as a proven fact, that following an alleged slight to French pride during the last war, any boat flying the Red Ensign is liable to be stoned by the locals – as though the French have far to look for reasons to resent the British (or us them, for that matter). Even on the Canal itself, after we had left the shallower water of the Canal du Midi for the Canal Latéral, several British boats heading south told us categorically that we'd never make it to Bordeaux.

We were intending to return to the UK from Croatia, where we'd spent the previous three years based in Dubrovnik. Our boat was a 43ft (13m) sailing boat, which is large or, rather, deep by the standards of the Canal. But with its "shoal" keel it draws just 1.5 metres – just within the theoretical limits of the Canal. Before deciding upon our route, I put out a request for information onto the Cruising Association website and found the response initially overwhelmingly negative. Several people who'd travelled the Canal on smaller boats reported touching bottom frequently. One had given up after they encountered shallow water in the Étang de Thau, and told me categorically that we'd never make it. I had almost abandoned the idea when we received an email from someone who'd actually been through with a boat drawing almost the same as ours. We decided that the only thing to do was to find out for ourselves.

The Canal du Midi itself is one of the narrowest and shallowest in France. It is therefore perhaps hardly surprising that its reputation has evolved as a small, meandering canal suitable only for little boats. Meandering it certainly is, but when you have seen the size of the commercial barges that it was designed to take, you will rapidly re-evaluate your idea of what is small. These things are huge, so huge that it seems impossible that they could even get past the next bridge. But they do. The situation is circular. Because few deeper-draught boats use the Canal, there is relatively little reliable information on its limitations. As a result even fewer people try it. Even when keel boats do go through, the Canal authorities are unlikely to be aware of – and cannot therefore be certain of – the *actual* depth restrictions. It's like a game of Chinese whispers; but reported advice is no substitute for first-hand experience.

Having once decided to try the Canal, we then realised that we simply had no idea what to expect. Many boats, well within the limits of the canal and intending to go out of season, can confidently look forward to an easy, trouble-free passage. For a sailing boat the first question is: Where can we take down the mast? Where can we put it back up again? For a motor boat, the question is unlikely to be the water draught, but the air draught. Others might be intending to hire a boat locally. But the fundamental problems still remain: What will we find when we get there? How much time is needed? How should we pace ourselves? How to organise crew changes? How to provision the boat?

This booklet is not intended to be a detailed guide: I have deliberately presented it as a narrative in an attempt to make it more readable. But within those limits, I have tried to cover the fundamentals of the Canal in order to give an idea of what to expect, as well as to highlight the historical and engineering importance of this magnificent waterway. My aim is to make people aware, not only of the benefits of the Canal as a passage to more distant places, but of its charm as a destination in itself.

The Canaux du Midi, perhaps because of their long history, are unlike the other canals in Europe. Each section is a discrete passage on its own and each has a clear personality and atmosphere significantly different from the others. The flat coastal land around the Étang de Thau and the associated routes through to the sea; the ancient Canal du Midi itself, redolent of a vanished pastoral trade and community; the Canal Latéral à la Garonne: larger, more industrial, perhaps more impersonal, more of a by-pass skirting the unreliable Garonne; the navigable, tidal river inland of Bordeaux, which passes through the heart of the Sauternes vineyards; and then the flatness of the vast Gironde estuary, with its fierce currents and muddy, eddying waters.

When we finally left Pauillac and set sail for Royan at the mouth of the Gironde estuary, our feeling was not one of relief at having made it successfully. It was of regret at what we were leaving behind us.

The Route

The Canal du Midi is just one of the waterways linking Royan, at the mouth of the Gironde estuary, to Sète, the official end of the original Canal on the Mediterranean. The route comprises four separate waterways: the Gironde estuary, the Garonne river, the Canal Latéral à la Garonne and the Canal du Midi. The complete crossing is known as the Canal des Deux Mers and comprises:

La Gironde:
Estuary from Royan to Bordeaux   100 km of tidal waters

La Garonne:
Bordeaux to Castets-en-Dorthe   54 km of tidal river

Canal Latéral à la Garonne:
Castets-en-Dorthe to Toulouse   193 km, 53 locks; all single-basin

Canal du Midi:
Toulouse to Sète   240 km, 63 locks; 11 double,
                                       4 triple, 1 4-basin, Fonsérannes

Before reaching Sète, two further waterways join the Canal du Midi, allowing access from the western ports of the Golfe du Lion:

Canal de la Robine:

Canal du Midi to Port-la-Nouvelle   36 km, 12 locks

L'Herault River:

Canal du Midi to Agde   5 km; 3-way lock into canal

Leaving Sète for the east is the **Canal du Rhône à Sète**, linking the Étang de Thau through the Camargue to the Rhone canals and to the sea at **Port St Louis du Rhône**. Intermediate access is possible through **Frontignan,** 1 km north of Sète.

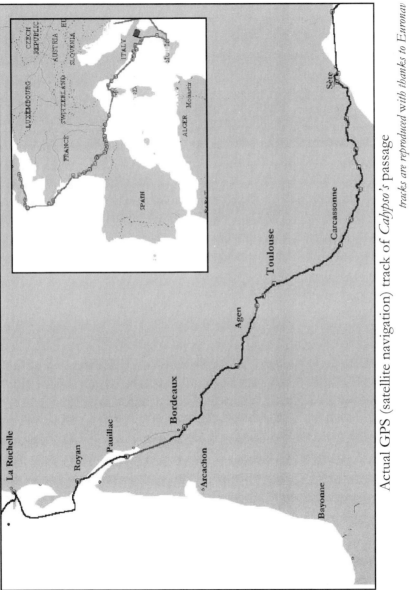

Actual GPS (satellite navigation) track of *Calypso's* passage

tracks are reproduced with thanks to Euronav

A Little History

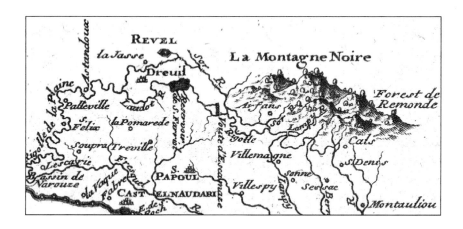

A short cut between the Atlantic and Mediterranean had been talked about almost since medieval times. It had long been seen as an affront to the French national pride that, to travel between their Atlantic and Mediterranean shores, ships had to pass through seas controlled by Spain. A canal would therefore not just benefit trade, but would also be an enduring symbol of France's military power. On a practical level, the existing ports on France's western Mediterranean coast had become silted up and too shallow to be of much use, and a new deep-water port would provide a valuable alternative to Marseille.

The concept of a canal wasn't as improbable as it might seem. The Garonne river is seasonally navigable from the Gironde estuary on the Atlantic, right up to Toulouse. From there to the Mediterranean, a distance of barely 150 km, there's a low-lying corridor leading to

17

Carcassonne and the coastal plains fringing the Golfe du Lion. The highest point, at Naurouze, is just 190 metres above sea level. The insuperable problem, however, was a source of water reliable enough to operate a canal.

It was Pierre-Paul Riquet, from an aristocratic family in Béziers, who found the solution. His father, a lawyer, was already a rich man, but his son added substantially to the family's fortunes when he was installed as administrator of the lucrative salt tax in the town of Revel. This put him in a position of considerable influence, enabling him to diversify his business interests and amass a fortune estimated to exceed a million livres from a contract to supply the armies of the King in Catalonia. During the many years he spent in Revel his interest in the idea of a canal grew, and eventually he became obsessed with finding a solution to the problem of a dependable water supply. Although he had no technical training, he carried out detailed investigations of the streams of the nearby Montagne Noire, often taking with him a local fountain designer, Pierre Campmas. It was from these visits that the idea slowly emerged that if he could harness the water from the numerous small streams and torrents running down from the mountain, then the water could be stored in a series of reservoirs which, in turn, could be led to a canal at the Col de Naurouze, the watershed between the two seas.

Riquet approached Colbert, *contrôleur général* under King Louis XIV of France, who was immediately sympathetic to the idea. Colbert considered that the only way to finance the Sun King's extravagance and balance the nation's books was to develop trade. International trade and the status of France had become almost indistinguishable in his mind, and he recognized the need for a good transportation network to connect France's industries to the sea. Construction of the Canal would create one of the largest civil engineering projects of its time, and this must also have added to its appeal for Colbert, who had recently become convinced that scientific discoveries could be used to boost trade and add to the glory of France. In 1666, the same year that he established the Académie Royale des Sciences, Colbert finally obtained Royal assent for Riquet's plans.

Riquet was already approaching 60 when, in 1667, over 12,000 people, women as well as men, finally started work. In spite of the huge sums of money required, his commitment to it was total. When questioned about the wisdom of risking his children's inheritance by embarking on this massive project at such an advanced age, he replied, "*I regard my work as the dearest of my children.*"

It was not just the design and construction of the canal that showed Riquet's brilliance, but also the innovative working practices he introduced. Although many of these have since been accepted as standard, at the time they created considerable enmity among other, less enlightened employers. His wages were above average, and paid monthly without deductions for public holidays or weekends. Neither was there any deduction for days lost when it rained, or when a worker was ill.

Work started first on the three dams which were to supply the canal. The first of these, the Bassin de St Ferréol, held nearly 7 million cubic metres of water – more than the entire capacity of the canal – and for a considerable time it was the largest man-made barrage ever built. Thereafter work started on the canal itself, starting in both directions from Trèbes, 12 km downstream of Carcassonne. On each section work started simultaneously at various points along the route, in order to speed the process. A third section was added when it was decided to abandon the original idea of going through the river Aude to join the sea at Narbonne. Problems with silting made them decide instead to extend the canal through the Étang de Thau to finish at Sète. The final section of work was therefore the construction of the port facilities at Sète itself.

But Riquet never saw the canal finished. He died aged just over 70 (his exact age is unknown), when there was only 3 km left to complete. Just seven months after his death, on 15th May 1681, The Canal Royal des Deux Mers was finally inaugurated by a procession of barges travelling along the 240-kilometre waterway, passing from the Garonne River at Toulouse to the Mediterranean at Sète. The two seas were finally joined.

During its construction Riquet made numerous breakthroughs. The Pont-Canal du Répudre was only the second canal viaduct in the world, and the first in France, while the tunnel of Malpas was the first built anywhere. The nine consecutive lock basins at Fonsérannes, avoiding the regular flooding of the Orbe River, were its most stunning achievement. The now-familiar olive-shaped locks (reputedly based upon an original Roman design) were adopted as the standard throughout the Canal in 1669, the only exception being the three-way circular lock at Agde, which offered an alternative access to the Mediterranean along the l'Hérault river.

The Canal aroused considerable admiration (or, depending upon the point of view, envy) on the other side of the Channel. Flattering reports in the journal of the Royal Society led one correspondent to berate the editor for praising French ingenuity at a time when such praise might dishearten the English who were (yet again) fighting in France – although I've no idea what it was about this time.

Improvements and alterations were made continually over the following centuries; the lock-keepers' cottages were added in the 18th century, while the principal lock outside Toulouse railway station was reconstructed just a few years ago. Following persistent problems with droughts during the 1970s and 1980s, the Canal became too unreliable as a source of water for irrigation of local fields and since the Montagne Noire had no more reserves of water, a fifth reservoir, the Montbel, was added twelve years ago in the Pyrenées to the west.

Immediately after Riquet's death, during the period from 1686 to 1693, the ubiquitous Vauban took over control of the works and added further engineering innovations, including more than 50 viaducts. The route of the canal also changed – Carcassonne, for example, which originally refused to contribute to the costs, relented soon after the canal's opening and the canal was re-routed through the centre. Vauban said of the enterprise: *"[it] is, without contradiction, the most beautiful and noble work of its kind ever undertaken . . . I would prefer the glory of having been the author of this, rather than all that I have ever done or might do in the future."*

In spite of the need to tranship most of the freight from the river barges of the Gironde at Toulouse to the smaller boats of the Mediterranean, the canal was an immediate commercial success, the most common cargoes being oil, wine, leather and Toulouse textiles. At its peak in 1856, just before the railway took over, it carried over 110 million tonnes of freight.

But its construction nearly ruined Riquet, and when he died his estate was deeply mortgaged and his children's inheritance almost exhausted. His two sons continued to represent the family's interests until finally, in 1724, they started to see a return on the investment. As the Canal slowly started to pay its way, Riquet's foresight as a financier became apparent. Although his contribution amounted to 2 million livres, the États de Languedoc and the Trésor Public had themselves put up the bulk of the huge cost, estimated at a further 16 million livres. In spite of this, Riquet's family was entitled to all the profit. But a century later, following construction of a new railway line running for much of its length alongside the canal (most recently joined by the main A61 motorway), the commercial viability of the canal was inevitably doomed. It rapidly lost customers, and in 1858 Riquet's descendants were forced to grant the Compagnie des Chemins de Fer an exclusive 40-year lease, with only a small annual payment to the family. The Company had recently completed the Canal Latéral from Toulouse to Bordeaux and now had a monopoly over the entire Languedoc transportation routes. It promptly raised canal prices to favour the railway, and the Canal's fortunes never recovered. The Canal was eventually taken over by the French government in 1898. The last commercial boat passed through in 1979 and finally, in 1996, its historical importance was recognised when it was classed as a UNESCO World Heritage site.

Using a dam built at Moussoulens, several attempts were made to canalise the Robine river as an alternative route to the sea, passing through Narbonne, but it could never supply enough water. It was nearly a hundred years later, following the construction of a fourth reservoir – the Lampy in the Black Mountains – that a reliable water supply became available and the link could finally be completed. The *Nouvel Embranchement* comprises the **Canal de la Robine,** which joins Port-la-Nouvelle with the Aude River in Moussoulens, and the **Canal de Jonction,** linking the Aude with the Canal du Midi at Port la Robine.

The rather prosaically named **Canal Latéral à la Garonne** had also formed part of Riquet's original dream, since not only was the Gironde River difficult to navigate, but it couldn't be used by boats from the Canal du Midi, requiring all cargoes to be transhipped at Toulouse. Several proposals were put forward during the eighteenth century, but it was not until 1832 that a new company was given the concession to build a canal. This company soon went bankrupt and the project was rescued only by an exceptional grant of 40 million francs from the government. After five years' work, the money again ran out, and questions were now being asked as to why the government should subsidise a canal to run alongside the new railway line – it was even suggested that the completed sections should simply be filled in. Eventually, in 1852, a 99-year concession was granted to the Compagnie des Chemins de Fer du Midi, whose new railway was already putting the Canal du Midi itself under severe competitive pressure. The first section of the Canal de Garonne to Montech had been opened in 1844 and the section to Castets-en-Dorthe was eventually completed in 1856.

The entire waterway is now administered by the VNF – the Voies Navigables de France.

Chapter One

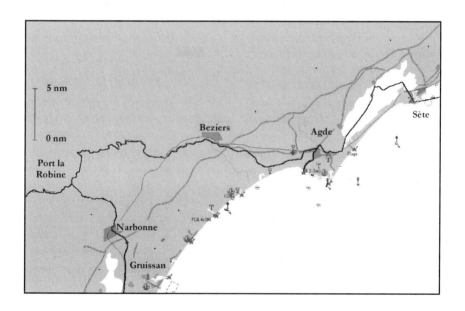

In the spring of 2002, my reason temporarily deserted me and I decided to order a new boat. Corinne, my wife and not-always-compliant crew, doesn't mince her words when she questions whether it's ever returned. As she pointed out, I had done nothing about selling our current boat, so where was the money going to come from?

Other writers have managed to buy boats from the proceeds of their writing. In 1948 George Millar bought an old boat with the funds and freedom provided by his first book, *Maquis*, the story of his time spent fighting with the French Resistance towards the end of the war. *"I wrote a very bad book, at a time when there were few other distractions and when people's judgements were warped; all the money I made from that book is going into the boat."* This was the first boat to go through the French canals immediately after the war in 1945. Afterwards, they sailed on to Greece, even writing a second book about it: *Isabel and the Sea.* Jonathan Raban managed the same sort of thing in order to buy *Gosfield Maid,* on which he wrote his travel narrative *Coasting.* Hillaire Belloc was another, with *Nona,* published in 1925.

It was unlikely, though, that the proceeds from *Caesar's Passage* would stretch very far. P.G. Wodehouse observed that publishing a first novel is like dropping a rose petal down the Grand Canyon of Arizona and waiting for the echo, so I wasn't planning to hang around to listen out for it. My book was being published in June and I wanted to disappear immediately afterwards – it had to learn to stand on its own feet and I didn't want to be there if it stumbled. After a couple of bookshop readings, I reckoned it would all be over by the beginning of July and I arranged with yacht brokers in Lymington to deliver *Calypso* in time for their used-boat show early in September. From her berth in Dubrovnik in the Adriatic, it was a passage of nearly 3,000 miles around the Iberian peninsula, but to achieve it in time without long passages at sea, there was no alternative but to try to cut through using the Canal du Midi.

For most people, the Canal is likely to be their gateway to, rather than from, the Mediterranean. The sunshine, the balmy waters, the adventures, would be all ahead of them. For us, it was the other way around. Four years earlier we had taken *Calypso* down along the Portuguese coast to Gibraltar, and then cruised around Spain, France and Italy. For the last three years we had wintered the boat in Croatia. So now we had to bring her back home and try to find her a new owner.

I'd started sailing when I was eleven and had owned a succession of boats. Corinne had known nothing about sailing, and was prepared to trust in my experience – I can think of no other explanation. *Calypso*, a Moody Eclipse 43, had been in our ownership for eight years, although it often seemed the other way around. She's our third Moody, and at the time we bought her she was the flagship of their fleet: a wheelhouse cruiser, which allows the boat to be steered from inside the cabin, keeping out of the wind and rain of northern Europe, or the sun of the south. Most importantly, it meant that when the passage was complete, instead of descending into a dark and claustrophobic hull, we could sit around the table and look out at the places it had taken such effort to reach. It also proved to be an excellent canal boat.

Fortunately, it also matched almost exactly what Corinne thought a boat should be. Sensibly, she has little patience with discomfort, and recognises with disarming honesty what most of us try hard to conceal. The sea is frightening. If she is to go on it, she wants it calm, sunny, warm and blue, with a five-day weather forecast that would make even the lobsters abandon their rocky depths for a swimming holiday on the surface.

In spite of this, I found myself looking forward to being in the Atlantic again, even if Corinne wasn't. We knew southern Brittany well, although we'd never been into La Rochelle itself – the last traditional harbour on the way south. From the UK to the secure locked basin in the centre of this stunning old fortified town is an easy week in good weather. Whether motoring, motor-sailing, or enjoying favourable winds, the passage from the Chénal du Four or Camaret down the southern Brittany coast can be made comfortably in four, day-long legs of between fifty and sixty miles, with attractive and secure overnight stops at Bénodet, Belle Isle and Ile d'Yeu. A fifth day takes you down to the entrance to the Gironde itself, and then up the estuary to Pauillac – probably the most convenient place to step or unstep the mast – just twenty miles beyond that. The last passage can be broken at Royan, tucked just inside the mouth of the estuary, where a boat can wait for the tide to turn up-river.

I hadn't realised that the Mediterranean could be so easily reached. Book a week's holiday and take the boat from the UK down to Les Minimes marina in La Rochelle, and fly back with Buzz (assuming Ryanair hasn't shut it down). Go out again in the summer and the Mediterranean is just two weeks away through the canals. From the UK to the Mediterranean in three weeks, with no more than a single night spent at sea? It seemed almost too good to be true.

To find out whether it was really that simple, I contacted André Fromilhague, the Cruising Association's representative in Bordeaux, who took the project in hand as though it were his own trip and contacted the various local offices of the VNF for their advice about the depth. Their response, however, was lukewarm, for although they said it was not *im*possible, they declined to take any responsibility for our decision. It was still only early spring, so we didn't have to decide just then, and André agreed to keep the situation under review while I went back to preparations for my book.

A month later I received a fax forwarded by André. It was a notice from the VNF that due to lack of water, the official level of the canal had been lowered from 1.6m to 1.4m. I telephoned him to ask whether the situation was likely to change by the summer and he said that the VNF's view was that it would be a "miracle" if there were to be enough rain over the next few months to recharge the reservoirs. Well, that seemed to be that. It was the long way around, whether we liked it or not.

I suppose bad weather is a mixed blessing. The summer of 2002 was poor across most of Europe, but in the Midi during late spring, it was atrocious. Eventually, in May, the VNF announced that they had lifted their restrictions and confirmed that the depth was now back to normal – nominally 1.6m (see Appendix). It was the near-biblical miracle we had been waiting for. After that, we had to try it.

Our journey started, incongruously enough, in Hackney. While the informal arrangement of a Helmsman's Overseas Certificate of

Competence is good enough for coastal waters, for some reason a written test – the *Code Européen des Voies de la Navigation Intérieure* (CEVNI) is needed to go inland. The RYA, who administer the test in the UK, had put me in touch with Paul, my nearest approved examiner, but as I rang the bell outside an anonymous block of flats in a residential street in Hackney, I thought there must have been a mistake. When the door was finally opened by a man in his dressing gown, his blank look almost convinced me that I was in the wrong place until it turned out that Paul had simply forgotten that I was coming. After I'd taken the test – I had to help mark it since he told me he'd never even been on an inland waterway in his life – Paul explained that his shore-based courses were generally given to groups in their own offices mainly based in the City of London, just down the road. But as I walked through the urban Hackney streets clutching my new CEVNI certificate, I couldn't help feeling vaguely disorientated.

Corinne couldn't leave until the middle of July, so we arranged that she would fly to Catania in Sicily while George and I set off from Dubrovnik to meet her there. George, the six-foot-three son of friends of ours, was having a gap year before going up to University the following autumn. He's a fanatical sailor and although I explained that sticking to deadlines in the Mediterranean normally meant more motoring than sailing, he was broad-minded about it. He was, however, worried about my computerised navigation system and insisted that I buy a set of paper charts. There are times when no one is more conservative than the young.

It was uneventful to Sicily and Corinne arrived as arranged. On our way through the Straits of Messina it was obligatory to put into Santa Maria la Scala, which, from our previous visits to Sicily, we knew had a home-made ice cream parlour without peer. Corinne and George hopped onto the quay and came back with a selection of fresh lemon, almond, blackberry, strawberry, peach and apricot ice creams that left even me silent for fifteen minutes.

Our son Chris was joining us in a few days, and had booked with Go (now part of Easyjet), flying into Naples, the most convenient route for a crew change in southern Italy. There are shuttle buses from the airport to Naples railway station, and from there the main line runs down the coast as far as the Golfo di Policastro, making any of the ports along its route easily accessible by express train. We dropped George off at the station in Agropoli – he was going cross-country to get a ferry back to his mother's house in Hvar in Croatia – and Corinne and I then meandered further up the coast, looking for somewhere to wait for Chris. Rejecting Salerno as being too commercial, we popped in Cetara a few miles to the west, to find it completely rebuilt and quite unlike its uncomplimentary description in our pilot book. The southern coastline of Italy is generously sprinkled with new ports built with development funds from the EC. Few of them have ever been finished, the money having trickled away like water through sand. Cetara was different because it was a fishing port rather than a marina, and was home to some huge tunny boats – although given the state of fish stocks, it might be a better idea to subsidise the fish rather than the fishermen. They'd recently installed a new pontoon where we spent a couple of days, but doubtless in a year's time this will have filled up with the usual collection of motley, little-used local boats, which pay only a subsidised rate and clog up so many Mediterranean harbours. We took a bus into Salerno and met Chris at the station. The next day we retraced our steps to visit Pompeii.

After that we island-hopped. In Capri we visited La Mortella, Sir William Walton's villa, where Lady Walton has established a magnificent, sub-tropical garden in the grounds looking west over the Tyrrhenian Sea. Then Ischia, Ventotene, Ponza, and an overnight passage to the island of Giglia, beyond Rome. Leaving Italy at Elba we crossed from Corsica to Porquerolles on the Isles d'Hyère, finally returning to the mainland west of Marseille, on the edge of the Rhone delta.

Our passage had given me plenty of time to worry about whether we would get through the Canal and, as we approached its entrance at Sète, I didn't know which concerned me more: running irretrievably aground somewhere in the middle of a French field, or not being able to take the mast down in the first place. In addition to all the various stays, I counted eleven separate electrical cables connecting the various paraphernalia on the mast. Even if I could get everything down successfully, would I ever get it reconnected again?

Sète, France's second port of the Western Mediterranean, is a place where yachts are tolerated rather than welcomed. Some of its fishing boats appeared to be the size of small cruise liners and we had to scurry out of their way as they charged straight at us to drop their catch at the fish market. A yacht can't buy any diesel either – or rather *we* couldn't, since the automatic pump accepts only French credit cards. There's an alternative fuel quay at Frontignan, just a mile or so to the north, which also allows access to the canal system and has its own mobile-crane operator who lives and works locally. But I estimated that diesel consumption on the canal shouldn't be very high, and leaving the tank only a third full would mean the boat would float higher in the water – I thought we probably had just enough to get us to Toulouse.

Sète's yacht pontoons are rather ramshackle affairs, and I looked in vain for the smart travel lift one finds in most French marinas. Instead, away from the market, tucked into a corner of the harbour, we saw a dilapidated boatyard and, sitting underneath its rusting crane, was an old man with a tattered cap. As we moored alongside, a couple of bloodshot eyes peered at us through a huge white beard and we noticed with alarm the substantial pile of discarded beer cans next to him. I started to doubt yet again whether this was a good idea, although I relaxed a bit when I discovered that at least he wasn't the crane driver. But without Hugo I don't see how we would have managed. He was a professional skipper on a nearby English yacht, and when we'd asked to borrow his bosun's chair he brought it over himself and then stayed on to help. After that everything happened so fast that I didn't have time to think about it. He immediately stopped me unloosening the shroud bottle screws before I had first wound tape around the threads to provide a mark for restepping the mast. To my enormous mortification, after I had clumsily and laboriously gone up in the bosun's chair to fix the crane's hook, when it later became caught he cradled the mast with his hands and simply walked up. I pretended I hadn't noticed, but afterwards I was happy to leave him to direct operations and he soon had the mast down and lashed. It was the ugly duckling in reverse, and it took us many days to adjust to the change. In just a couple of hours *Calypso* had changed from an elegant sailing yacht into some kind of floating battering ram, with our mast jutting out ahead of us and rigging trailing along the decks.

It was now time for Chris to leave us. Once again taking advantage of the revolution provided by low-cost airlines, he booked a flight to London from Montpellier for around eighty pounds. When we used to live in the south of France in the seventies, flying there was, mile for mile, one of the most expensive air routes in the world. Now we were almost spoilt for choice: Toulon, Marseille, Montpellier, Carcassonne. There's even a direct TGV rail connection from Sète to Paris and then on to Waterloo, with heavily discounted fares if you're under twenty-five. After Chris had left for the airport, Corinne and I walked slowly back from the station, subdued by his absence. We had enjoyed more than two weeks of his company, and not only did the boat not feel the same without him: it wasn't the same.

Ironically, although Sète owed its earlier prosperity to its position at the entrance to the Canal du Midi (its main thoroughfares are canals), its bridges are too low for most boats to pass under. Although it's possible to make special arrangements, there are only two scheduled openings each day, so it wasn't until that evening, with our mast lashed to the deck, that we finally passed through into the Étang de Thau.

The Canal proper starts at the other end of the Étang, which is one of a series of saltwater lagoons lying behind the coast between Marseille and the Spanish border, created by the silt carried from the Rhone delta. They were just mosquito-ridden swamps until the French Government recognised their tourist potential in the sixties and created the string of modern marina villages (of varying degrees of ugliness) which now line the coast. The opening bridges at Sète make it possible to go inland without taking the mast down, and a number of yachts are kept on moorings inside the Étang – or even in the start of the canal itself. The old fishing villages of Mèze and Marseillan have small ports and even petrol pumps (but no diesel), while passage along the Canal is possible for 2 km until reaching the first road bridge.

There's a strange feeling of limbo entering the lagoon. It's big – ten miles long – and has a strange life of its own; a sort of halfway house, neither sea nor canal. We spent the night anchored off Meze, and our last night in open water was an eerie experience – the shadowy outlines of the countless rows of oyster beds stretched into the gloom until the dark, still water merged into the night.

Chapter Two

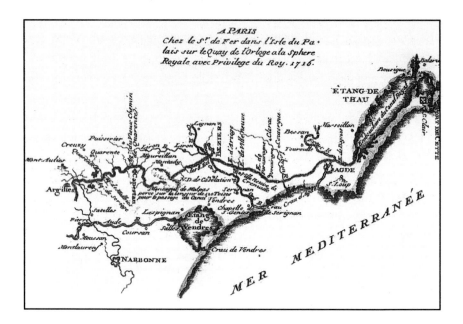

In spite of the warnings, we encountered no problems in the Étang de Thau. In Mèze (which is marked as having a depth of only 1m), even approaching the canal there was never less than 2 metres, and usually much more. I suspect, though, that even this must come as a shock to many yachtsmen who, after several years in the Mediterranean, are not accustomed to seeing such low readings on their echo sounder.

The next morning we entered the canal proper. Although we had been told that the boat would float several inches lower in fresh water, I could detect no difference in our waterline, perhaps because of her hull shape, and we were reassured that, at least at first, we rarely seemed to have less than half a metre of water under our keel. It was strange to be travelling so close to the invisible sea just the other side of the low sand spits, but access to the beaches of the Mediterranean makes this stretch of the canal a particularly attractive destination.

One of the largest of the boat-hire companies, Crown Blue lines, has its substantial southern base here at Port Cassafières (PK222) and, apart from servicing their own boats, they also sell diesel from a pump on the banks and can even provide a mechanic when they're not busy. Crown Blue has two bases on the Canal, as well as operations on the Lot and Baïse rivers, with other operations spread throughout Europe and, most recently, in the United States. Originally established in 1969 as Bateaux Bleus by an enterprising Brit, Michael Street, who brought eight boats down from the Norfolk Broads on a lorry, the business thrived and he eventually sold out to the Rank Organisation. By 1990 it had 400 boats and was then taken over by the much smaller Crown Cruisers, a company with just 100 boats. Crown Blue retained its headquarters in Norwich until very recently, but after yet another takeover it's now part of the First Choice group (which has also just added Connoisseur lines to its fleet), and their offices have been relocated to the South Coast, alongside sister company, Sunsail.

Ironically, while all its boats are still manufactured by a subsidiary near Lowestoft which turns out about fifty a year – mainly of the newer Andrew Wolstenholme-designed *Classique* – Crown Blue have never operated on the Broads themselves. Although production of the original and distinctive blue boats stopped over twenty years ago, they remain very popular with renters, and every year a couple of the fleet are sold off, where they still attract prices of up to £20,000. Their flat-bottomed hull also makes them an excellent boat for exploring drying tidal waters, and we later saw one lying incongruously on the mud in an otherwise deserted reach of the Tamar above Plymouth.

With a typically pragmatic and reliably inconsistent Gallic logic, the French authorities have waived the requirement for a CEVNI licence for people hiring boats. Pragmatic because otherwise the boat-hire business would immediately collapse; utterly inconsistent because it means that only a tiny minority of boaters on the Canal actually possess the qualification that, for safety reasons, is supposed to be obligatory. Perhaps it would be easier if they simply abolished it.

The only landmark ahead was the prominent town of Agde, built on a dark volcanic hill at the mouth of l'Hérault river and one of the oldest settlements of the Western Mediterranean. The river joins the canal in an extraordinary circular lock, enabling barges to be rotated inside it: a sort of turntable that allows boats either to continue straight ahead along the Canal, or to turn and take the alterative route to the sea through Agde. From each of these three directions came an extraordinary selection of polyglot boats, and this was to be the feature of the next couple of weeks.

Ninety-five percent of these boats are hired from one of several rental companies based on the Canal. Coming from around the world, their crews were all determined to enjoy their holidays and the atmosphere was relaxed and friendly, even though some were – to put it politely – inexperienced. We watched with increasing amazement as one rental boat bounced backwards and forwards off the round walls of the lock, completely unable to understand the effect of the steering wheel. Bits of tangled GRP were left behind after each impact, sticking out randomly from the cracks of the stonework. The lock-keeper appeared completely unfazed; I suppose she had seen it all countless times before, but for us it was a preview of what lay ahead. We were travelling in August and were under no illusions about how busy it was going to be, but we had no choice – we had to be back in the UK for the boat show. What I hadn't expected, however, were boats that seemed to spend most of their time virtually out of control. A purpose-designed boat, carrying a string of continuous fixed fenders or surrounded by thick rubbing strakes like a dodgem at a funfair, is well protected. But when on your own boat, you simply have to carry lots of fenders (tyres are prohibited because they don't float) and stay ready for sudden, random and incomprehensible manoeuvres. If there are four or more boats in the lock, as there were for us most of the time, it could become quite wearing, particularly if there were any cross-winds, which could add enormously to the excitement. At least it was nearly always good-natured.

Villeneuve-les-Béziers (PK 214) was celebrating its carnival with waterborne jousting tournaments when we arrived. This meant that we couldn't explore the restaurants marked a stone's throw from the canal. While waiting for a bout to end, we held on alongside a traditional old barge which turned out to be a charter boat with an English crew. The young skipper's parents were English, but he had been brought up on their boat in the north of France and was bilingual. There were two "chalet girls" who did the catering and a third who went on ahead in a people carrier to buy supplies or arrange various visits along the way. They were waiting for their new guests – two couples from the States who were obviously about to spend a very pampered week aboard.

Jousting is a sport found throughout the French canals, as well as in the harbours of the south. Two boats, each propelled by a dozen oarsmen, face one another while a jouster armed with a lance balances himself on a raised platform at the back. At a signal the boats head for one another, passing with a clashing of oars and hopefully leaving one of the jousters floundering in the water. It seemed to us that the incentive to keep dry was quite powerful, since there are no pump-out facilities anywhere on the canal, leaving every boat no choice but to discharge its toilets directly into the water. In spite of this, not once did we hear anyone even referring to the problem, and neither did it seem to bother the commune of Villeneuve. They had erected a temporary stand on either side of the canal, the locals were obviously warming up for a long day, and clearly didn't want their enjoyment to be interrupted by passing boats or by concerns about the water quality. They even tried to wave us back, suggesting that the canal was closed, but we could see that a boat ahead was waiting to enter the lock just beyond the bridge. I didn't fancy spending the entire day there, so when the lock gates opened, I gave the engine a quick burst and nipped past the stands between jousts.

To be fair to hire boats, keeping a steady course through the canals is surprisingly difficult and I'm still not quite sure why. I think it's partly the unfamiliar narrowness of the waterway – when mooring up in a marina there's usually plenty of room to forgive mistakes. It's also partly to do with the effect of the displaced water – an Autohelm can easily keep a rock-steady course at sea, but on a straight canal it soon begins to oscillate. Bridges, however, were an unfamiliar problem where the effect is most noticeable. Some are alarmingly narrow – Corinne refused point-blank to steer through any of them – and motoring through them at any speed is certainly nerve-racking. I then noticed that many of the bridges have a painted mark on the keystone and, by lining up the bows with the mark, you're guaranteed not to hit the walls. Guaranteed, that is, as long as there is no towpath under the bridge. If there is, then the centre of the waterway is no longer the centre of the bridge and things get more interesting (see drawing in the Appendix). It's not so bad if you have enough room to line up the boat in advance, but sometimes the bridges are adjacent to bends – it clearly needs a lot of skill to drive a commercial barge.

Going into locks is also surprisingly tricky. The slow speed makes steering difficult, especially if there's any wind, and if there's been a wait to enter the lock and you're starting from standstill, then at first the boat will not "track" properly. I hadn't expected to use it at all inland, but I found the bow-thruster invaluable in helping to line up the boat. Manoeuvring inside a narrow lock can also present a challenge, particularly when one half of the deck is completely obstructed by the mast.

The first of Riquet's masterpieces is the series of locks at Fonsérannes, across the valley from Béziers. Seven of the original nine consecutive basins remain, giving a rise of nearly 14 metres, and we approached anxiously. The sight of the water cascading down onto the boat from the sluice gates ahead is dramatic and alarming. It was bad enough for me in the cockpit at the stern, but for Corinne standing on the bows it was terrifying. There's a rule on all French canals that lifejackets must always be worn in the locks, but although no one would stand much chance in the churning water, the rule was universally ignored. Later we asked a VNF official if there were many accidental deaths on the Canal. 'Not this year,' she replied ominously. She added cheerfully that the seclusion of canals has always made them attractive as a place to dispose of bodies – either your own or other people's.

Boats pass through Fonsérannes in convoy, using several basins at once. This makes it a one-way system, and the day is divided into downstream and upstream periods. They're listed in the guide, and by luck we managed to time our arrival to avoid a long wait. But once you're in, there's no chance for a breather and it's tough going – although once again we had mercifully little opportunity to think about it as we worked our way inexorably upwards.

At the top, trembling from a combination of tiredness and relief, we decided to rest and visit the tourist office – once an old *auberge* – at the top of the locks. Along with its stables, it was the last lunch stop of the old *barque de poste*, where the boat took on passengers for Toulouse returning up-river, while the travellers bound for Agde joined another boat waiting below. It was the canal's answer to the stage-coach. The journey lasted four days, leaving Toulouse early, lunching by the Négra lock and spending the night in Castelnaudary. The next day the midday stop was at Béteille, and the night at Trèbes. Then lunch at La Redorte, with dinner at Somail. The last day, after Fonsérannes, passengers disembarked at Agde in the evening. It was generally considered safer and more comfortable than the coach and became remarkably popular. During its peak year, in 1856, it carried nearly 100,000 people, but shortly after that it succumbed to the competition from the new railway service built alongside.

We felt we had done enough for our first day. Underneath the overhanging trees it was starting to get dark. The next lock at Argens wasn't for another 54 km, offering us the prospect of an entire day without locks. We checked the map: Fonsérannes was located between PK207 and PK206 and there seemed to be a promising place just ahead of us. The PKs – Pointe Kilomètres – are the Canal's equivalent of milestones, although since most of the stones themselves are no longer in place, they generally exist simply as marks on the chart. The canal starts at PK240 at the entrance to the Étang de Thau and ends at PK0 in the Port de l'Embouchure in Toulouse, before counting back up to PK193 in Castets-en-Dorthe. It's the standard marking system throughout France and is even used on navigable rivers until they meet the sea.

As we tried to moor alongside the towpath a couple of kilometres past Fonsérannes (around PK203), we found ourselves running aground several yards off. When the mud has been lying around for over three centuries with nothing much to disturb it, an echo sounder can't tell you where it begins and ends. At what point does it change from muddy water to watery mud? We were still towing the tender and so I tied it between *Calypso* and the towpath, and for this and most subsequent nights it was our only way of getting ashore – even across a distance of only a couple of yards. Not having any mooring stakes, the tree roots lining the bank provided a useful mooring point. Force of habit then made me rig up an anchor light, although it took me several days to realise that with the locks shut, boats can't travel at night. The canal was now high up on a ridge, overlooking the river Orb. It was a beautiful night, calm and peaceful. Across the valley, floodlights shone on Béziers cathedral, illuminating it like a distant stage set.

Chapter Three

We decided to take time out the next day to visit the remains of an iron-age settlement, the Oppidum d'Enserune, on the top of a rocky outcrop through which Riquet built the world's first canal tunnel. The hill overlooks the Étang de Montady, a circular field several kilometres in diameter, divided into extraordinary pie-shaped segments. The medieval co-operative which first drained the lake still exists and cultivation rights can be traced back directly to the original share allocations made in 1247. It was a hot climb, but rewarded by a magnificent view across the lagoons surrounding Narbonne and towards the sea. At our feet, the tortuous course of the canal was marked by the densely packed plane trees which line its path. 45,000 of these trees were planted when the canal first opened, and they've since developed an almost symbiotic relationship with the canal – in return for its water, their interlocking roots protect its banks like a cocoon. Looking after the trees is as important as looking after the canal itself.

After visiting the strangely grand museum at the top, we came across the English barge crew whom we'd met the previous day while waiting for a break in the jousting tournaments. Their American guests had arrived safely and they'd been brought up in the people carrier. Did I detect a hint of smugness as they climbed into their air-conditioned vehicle, while we left them to scramble sweatily down the hill to rejoin our boat?

At Poilhes (PK194) we managed to moor alongside the quay where, unusually, there was 2m of water, and while Corinne went off to find some bread, I washed down the boat with a hose operated from a coin-in-the-slot machine – although €1 didn't go very far. With a couple of restaurants nearby, one (La Tour Sarasine) even makes Grade 12 in the Gault-Millau guide, it's a good place to stop for lunch or dinner, but unfortunately it was still too early and even though Corinne hadn't found a bakery, we pressed on and managed to buy some bread from a restaurant further along.

The next stretch after Capestang is narrow and winds tortuously around the contours of the Aude valley, just above the old Étang de Capestang across to the south. We generally tried to keep to the centre of the canal, indicating our draft to passing boats with sign language. Most obliged us by pulling over, some however, thought it was a game of chicken and stood on, while Corinne manned the fenders and closed her eyes. Occasionally the tables were turned when an old commercial barge approached from ahead, forcing us to pull into the side. Going round the numerous blind bends was particularly alarming, especially where the canal is narrow and the branches hang low over the water. We used the fog-horn frequently, although no one else seemed to, and our anxiety about meeting someone head-on (amplified by the fact that this anxiety appeared to be shared by no one else) frequently led us to slow almost to a stop before sharp bends.

The Canal de Jonction joins at Port la Robine (PK168), bringing boats from Narbonne, and a quick way to visit the city is to use the tourist railway running alongside it. I had originally intended to use this canal, and take the mast down at Port-la-Nouvelle, but when I realised that this would mean that we wouldn't complete the full length of the Canal du Midi, I had changed my mind. I wanted to do it all.

As each kilometre passed, we became increasingly confident that we were going to make it. But a British yacht was approaching from Toulouse. It was smaller than us but we called out to them anxiously, 'What's it like ahead?'

'Fine,' they replied as they passed. Moments later we came to a juddering halt as we ran straight into a mud bank. *All* advice needs to be treated with circumspection.

It was late afternoon by the time we reached Ventenac-en-Minervois (PK161) In retrospect we have should have stopped for the night near the bar and restaurant on the quayside, but we still didn't appreciate how few and far between these are. Shortly afterwards we crossed the small stream of le Repudre river, the first viaduct in France, and then moored for the night just beyond Paraza (PK157). Confident that we'd find at least a small bar in which to soak up some local atmosphere (not to mention some local aperitif), we returned later to Paraza in the dinghy, but found instead what appeared to be a ghost town and not for the first time promised to take advantage of the facilities when we passed them.

We had expected the canals to be lined with little villages, each with their own bistro, bar and boulangerie. Accustomed when in France to start the day with fresh bread and croissants, we were disappointed.

The Canal might be over three hundred years old, but the villages still predate it, and most are some distance from the canal. For this reason the hire boats are usually equipped with bicycles, but without them, if the villages weren't actually on the Canal, we would have to walk and there was no guarantee that we would find anything when we got there. We learnt that it was essential to buy supplies when we could. The following day we found the enterprising wife of the lock-keeper at the Argens lock (PK152/3) was selling fresh bread and local produce, but this was rare. A couple of times we managed to hail a passing bread delivery van, but generally we had to make do with toast in the mornings. There were also fewer canal-side restaurants than we had been expecting, but I suppose the lack of any close relationship between the Canal and the villages is hardly surprising. Except at major bases such as Castelnaudary and the stopping places of the *barque de poste*, the Canal would have brought little commercial benefit to the places it passed through. Even now it is busy only for the few summer months, and at other times a restaurant can't survive on the few customers the Canal can provide out of season.

We had plenty of time to eat the bread we'd bought at Argens since it took us an hour to get through, even though it's only a single basin. The time taken can vary enormously depending upon the number of boats waiting, the competence of their crews and their ability to handle their boat. The lock keepers use VHF radio to keep in touch the adjacent locks up- and downstream, and attempt to anticipate when boats are likely to arrive and from which direction. On our first day, where l'Herault river had joined us for a kilometre or so, we'd ventured towards the town centre for a look around before turning back to the round lock at Agde. But by the time we got there the gates had shut against us. The lock keeper told us she'd waited as long as she could, but a convoy of boats coming downstream was building up a queue on the other side. She estimated that we'd have to wait half an hour, but in fact it took twice as long because of the astonishing incompetence of some of the other crews. With hindsight we looked back upon the delay with some relief – the alternative would have been to share the lock with them.

The next lock, Pechlaurier (PK150-PK152) with two basins, took over two hours instead of about 25 minutes. We arrived just as the gates were closing against us, and there were four boats – a lock's complement – ahead of us. This meant we had to wait for two cycles, four separate passes, before we could even get in. Patience is essential and when it's busy it becomes very difficult to estimate just how long locks are likely to take. Further on, we passed through the four locks just before Castelnaudary in just a couple of hours, even though they contained a total of ten basins. On our second day, in spite of stopping to visit the Oppidum d'Enserune, there had been no locks and we travelled 28 miles. On our third day we only managed fourteen miles through eights locks, while on the fourth day we travelled nearly nineteen miles through eighteen locks. This uncertainty made pacing very difficult since we could never be sure how far we were likely to go in a day. As a result, when we arranged with our friends and London neighbours, Gill and Ian Jarvis, to meet them the following day for lunch, we had little idea where to tell them to go. Ian said he often visited the lock in the quaintly named village of Homps and suggested meeting there, but after a quick look at the guide I said we would we'd be far beyond it and crossed my fingers.

After Argens, the *biefs* were becoming quite short. (As far as I can tell *bief*, referring to the stretch between each lock, has no direct equivalent in English. It's loosely translated in the guides as a reach, which is not quite the same thing.) We were now finding locks every two or three kilometres, many of them doubles, or even triples. There are 63 locks between Sète and Toulouse, with over 100 separate basins, and excepting the few which have been replaced with modern concrete sides, virtually all the Canal du Midi locks retain the original olive shape. The advantage (to the canal operator) and the disadvantage (to you) is that although boats can enter only in single file, but once in they can lie side by side. In some double locks this is aggravated by the lock keeper allowing boats to travel in both directions at the same time – passing between the two basins at the halfway stage. This ambitious manoeuvre frequently results in complete chaos – but then so do the simple ones.

The curving walls also presented problems for our overhang mast. As the water rushed into the lock, our bows were forced against the wall, and it was only by Corinne pushing off with the boat hook that we managed to keep it from hitting the side. In one of the locks the force was too great and the mast hit the wall ahead of us and slid off the pulpit. Mercifully it came to rest on the guard wire. If it hadn't, it would have gone overboard and blocked the lock gates until a crane and a diver could be brought up – a cost I didn't even want to think about.

Although each lock has a keeper resident in the adjacent cottage (many are married women whose husbands work elsewhere) the advent of the 35-hour week has meant that during the summer many lock-keepers are students filling in for the lock-keeper's day off. They operate a rotation system allowing the stand-in to man (or woman?) different locks each day. In our experience both the students and the professional were, almost without exception, friendly and helpful. Do not, however, mistake this for a deep knowledge of the canals – few of them have ever been through the canal themselves and one told me she'd never even been on a boat. They will arrange the boats in a lock, but never let them decide how you should moor – that's your job and almost certainly you know more about it than they do. It's also your problem if anything goes wrong.

It was now becoming clear that we had been wildly optimistic when we had arranged our rendezvous with the Jarvises, and that had we known how long it would take, we could have arranged to meet at a small restaurant underneath the trees by the Ognon lock (PK147). Once again we had failed to take advantage of it as we passed – would we never learn? But it was too late; I wasn't going to turn around under any circumstances. Fortunately we were able to contact them by mobile phone and divert them back to Homps, as Ian had originally suggested. Of course that wasn't the only thing being diverted – a mobile phone call between two UK phones, both in France, is probably bounced between half a dozen satellites strung out around the globe. It certainly has a cost to match.

It turned out, of course, that there are three locks in Homps (one a double) and none of them was in the village itself. I had no idea which one Ian said he visits often, so we'd just have to carry on through them all until we met them. Three quarters of an hour later than arranged, Gill and Ian finally came on board, bringing along Daniel, their student son, who was with a college friend. I got the impression that they were all slightly bemused by the sight of our boat which, with its wires and cables hanging all around, hardly looked the elegant yacht that we had told them about. But as it started to rain, they certainly appreciated the cabin. Ian had been brought up in Hertfordshire and as a boy had spent a lot of time hanging around the canals and helping out with the locks. He was delighted to be back – it was as though he changed into that boy in front of our eyes, regressing through … well anyway, he was clearly thoroughly enjoying it all.

Daniel was less keen after he fell in – not uncommon on *Calypso* when visitors hold onto the hinged ladder on the transom, under the misapprehension it's fixed. Given the state of the water, I think he took it very well. On balance we decided against a stomach pump, but rushed him into a hot shower instead.

Our visitors only stayed for a couple of locks. I think as far as Daniel was concerned, his enthusiasm for the canals was somewhat dampened – as were his trousers, but we tentatively arranged to meet further on, after Carcassonne. Meanwhile the rain was getting harder and we decided to stop by l'Aiguille lock (PK133) where we retreated into the cabin, shutting the hatch firmly behind us. We closed the curtains and spent the evening reading and, while the rain hammered insistently on the coachroof, we complacently revelled in our comfortable and secure self-sufficiency.

We were slowly establishing a rhythm. We would be waiting at the first lock when it opened at nine, intending to carry on until they shut at seven o'clock. This being France, the lock keepers rigidly observed their lunch break and if we timed it right, we could eat at a canal-side restaurant – if we found one – while we waited. We were even managing better inside the locks. Although it was still impossible to get a rope onto the quay from the deck, we knew we could get help either from the lock keeper, or from one of the many spectators who were usually only too willing to become participants. With three people on board it would have been possible to drop a crew member to run up ahead and take lines, but with just the two of us, we needed help to go uphill. I was, however, making some progress and was starting to use a running moor – keeping the helm held hard over and the engine in gear pulling against a spring line. This pushed our bows out into the current and kept the mast away from the wall. Even so, Corinne still had to stand by to heave us off and for several months afterwards she would proudly display her muscles to anyone showing an interest.

The mast effectively turned our starboard side into a no-go area. The only way to get to it was to lie flat and wriggle underneath it and even then we would become trapped in the crevices formed by the spreaders, stays and stanchions. At least I was able to congratulate myself on having the foresight to leave the port side clear and this proved of vital importance. The paddle-wheel effect of our propeller meant that putting the engine in reverse kicked the stern across to port, making it much easier to come alongside – it would have been far more difficult with the mast on the other side.

The following morning Marseillette (PK127), just six kilometres ahead, looked promising with a long stone quay with a row of houses facing us. However there was absolutely no one about and, unfortunately, not the slightest sign of a *boulangerie*.

It was here at Trèbes (PK118) that construction of the canal first started and not surprisingly it provided one of the overnight stops for the old *barque de poste*. It still has a little restaurant in an old converted mill overlooking the lock, and it's a good idea to aim here for lunch so that if you have to wait for other boats, it can be done over a leisurely *café cognac*. Certainly the people sitting contentedly around the outdoor tables didn't seem in the least bit impatient to go anywhere.

As the Canal starts to climb away from the sea, it passes through the extensive vineyards of the Languedoc. One of the largest wine regions in the world, it had been in decline for many years and the wine was often fit only for industrial alcohol, but they're trying hard to re-establish the *appellations*, many of which are on sale outside the lock keepers' houses, displayed alongside other local produce. The seemingly unending rows of shimmering vines is one of the most attractive sights of the Canal, although after several days I was wondering who could be drinking quite so much of the wine (we were doing what we could to help out).

But the Canal was definitely becoming shallower. I could sense that although we weren't actually touching the bottom, our keel was now frequently pushing through the top of the soft mud. As we approached Carcassonne, tree roots lined the bottom like speed bumps, but we pressed on with the desperation of a car with a flat tyre trying to reach the service station just ahead. The towering walls of the ancient citadel that dominated the town and river to the west were just a distraction. Perhaps everyone else had been right. Perhaps we weren't going to make it after all.

Chapter Four

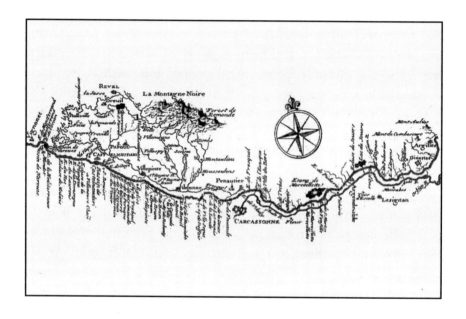

Of all the advice we had been given, no one had told us about the approach to Carcassonne. Given such a propensity of people to pass on bad news, I had assumed that we would have been made well aware of any problems which lay ahead of us, and so we'd been gaining confidence that the worst must be behind us. Whether the bumps were actually tree roots, or simply patches of harder mud, we had no means of telling, but I slowed right down and kept going until finally, with considerable relief, we entered the lock leading into the town's marina. It was now early evening and we decided that the next day could take care of itself. Getting this far was cause enough for celebration, so we went out for dinner. So far, so good – at least that's what the man said who jumped off the 20th floor as he passed the 10th.

It had been a long way since Dubrovnik, and the next day I decided it was time for an oil change. The marina is at the centre of the new town, directly opposite the station, so I thought we wouldn't find a better place to do it. Unfortunately the incredibly unhelpful woman in charge of the *Capitainerie* refused to understand that an ordinary motor mechanic could service a marine diesel, and insisted that there was no one in Carcassonne who could help us. After an extensive walk around the neighbourhood, I eventually discovered that there were several mechanics quite close to the marina – there was even one on the waterfront by the lock. The bad news was that most of them were on *fermeture annuelle*, and even when I found one still working he was too busy to come, leaving me with no choice but to do it myself. Fortunately he let me use his tank for the old oil and lent me his wrench to unscrew the oil filter. The garage was quite close, but by the time I'd done the round trip for the fifth time I was getting pretty frustrated – made worse by the fact that he didn't have any replacement filters and the only place I could get one was nearly two miles away. It was probably the only time anyone has walked a half-marathon while doing an engine service.

Somehow I've always managed without a hammer – the winch handle had always coped perfectly adequately. This time, however, it simply couldn't shift the oil cap to the gearbox, so Corinne walked around to the VNF maintenance depot next door to the *Capitainerie*. When she came back with a large hammer she was laughing. 'They asked me what you wanted to do with it,' she said. 'I told her that people in the Midlands call it a Birmingham screwdriver, so I said you could be doing just about anything.' She giggled. Apparently they'd made a few suggestions.

The large boat basin in Carcassonne is unusually deep, and we were able to lie alongside a pontoon and wash some of the mud off the hull. In spite of their berthing charges being surprisingly low, it's one of the best-equipped marinas of the canal, with water and electricity, as well as being the only place where we found washing and drying machines for our growing mound of dirty clothes. In the new town nearby there is a comprehensive range of shops, including several small supermarkets which will deliver directly to the boat. But one thing they did not have was a chandler. In fact we never saw one during the entire passage. Later, as I was washing down the boat, a colony of beavers swam over and started paddling happily around. They had escaped from a nearby fur farm some years ago and were surviving contentedly alongside the ducks, as eager as they were to grab any scraps of bread thrown from the boats.

Eventually our chores were completed. Clothes and boat washed, clean oil in the engine, knuckles scraped and scrubbed. It was time to do some sightseeing. We walked across to visit the medieval citadel.

I thought the canal had been busy, but Carcassonne was ridiculous. It had been heavily restored during much of the nineteenth century and in the process had lost much, if not all, of any medieval feeling. The façades were in such improbably good condition that it had the air of a film set; the hordes of people surrounding the many professional entertainers simply added to the illusion that we'd wandered into Disneyland by mistake. Much of the restoration formed the model for the Victorian additions at Windsor Castle, where the tower overlooking Eton bridge is a copy of the main tower in Carcassonne. Corinne, always a sucker for nostalgia, wanted to visit the hotel where she'd stayed with her grandparents as a girl. We wandered through its large public rooms, all decorated in an improbable Scottish Baronial style with severed deers' heads and crossed swords lining the oak-panelled walls. The manager told us proudly that it had been refurbished just a couple of years earlier. We decided not to stay for a drink.

It had been a tiring day off; our reunion with the canal the next day felt like meeting an old friend and we dropped quickly back into our routine. But we didn't get far, since the second lock was broken. The lock-keeper told us he thought he could fix it, but after half an hour he called in the maintenance team, who arrived from Carcassonne. As the mechanic took his toolbox from the back of his van, he waved across at Corinne who, reunited with her admirers from the previous day, called back, 'I hope you brought the screwdriver.'

While we waited, we got a call from Gill and Ian, and arranged to meet them for lunch. Gill agreed to take Corinne off in her car to stock up at a supermarket, while Ian and I continued ahead towards Castelnaudary. This time we'd learnt our lesson and didn't plan it in advance. We told them to call us when they were near and set off, as the mechanic opened the lock gates with a flourish and bowed towards Corinne as we passed. There was no sign of a hammer

I think this was the only time on the Canal du Midi (as opposed to the Canal Latéral) that we had to wait by a lock for a mechanic, but even when the lock was working normally we found hanging around for the gates to open surprisingly difficult. At first we had pulled into the bank and just rested on the bottom. But we soon noticed that the water level is constantly fluctuating and drops immediately after the gates have opened, if only by a few inches. But that is quite enough to turn what had been a gentle nudge into the mud into a major stranding, and we had to be careful about motoring off. Too much power simply buried the keel further in. We then discovered an alternative approach. Just like many river estuaries, the water leaving the lock produces a sill just downstream of it. Between this sill and the lock, for a distance of under a hundred yards, the bottom is scoured to create what is often quite a deep basin. This makes it possible to moor alongside the towpath, adjacent to the lock.

Although this gave Corinne the unusual opportunity to get ashore to buy provisions (if there were any to be had), or just wait alongside without worrying about grounding, the downside was that if there are people ahead of you, some of them might suspect that some queue jumping is going on. Although we were scrupulous in explaining what we were doing if we passed any waiting boats, one of them couldn't shake off the certainty that we were not waiting our turn. They simply couldn't understand what a keel is. They said that they too touched bottom when they went alongside, and they were quite incapable of appreciating the meaning of "draught", convinced that all boats must be the same under the waterline and all must therefore have the same problems. Unfortunately we had the misfortune to go through several locks with them. In spite of the fact that we diligently let them through first, and in spite of our repeated explanations, they spent the entire time insulting us and everything British, even managing somehow to bring the Queen into it. We tried everything, but there appeared to be absolutely nothing we could do to make them understand. Finally, we asked the lock-keeper to try and explain it to them, but instead he quickly shut the gates as soon as they had gone in, leaving us waiting outside. I think he'd been told by the previous lock-keeper of the tirade we had received, and had come to the conclusion that the easiest thing was simply to keep us apart. It was probably a good idea, since nothing else had worked.

After that we kept our distance and continued on towards Bram (PK81–83), where the reaches on either side are open and give a wonderful view across the fields. The Canal normally has an embankment running alongside the towpath, formed from the earth taken out by the original excavations. These banks, often quite high, add to the general feeling of privacy and seclusion, but if I were hiring a boat I'd make sure it had a flybridge, so that I could see as much as possible over them. This was one of the important features built in to Andrew Wolstenholme's designs for Crown Blue, although they're not such a good thing if it rains, as it now started to do with some force. Fortunately, even though the mast and stays obscured our view ahead, for most reaches I could steer from the wheel inside the cabin. We didn't mind the rain as much as we might have, because unbroken sunshine would become quite uncomfortable, showing up what is probably the major weakness of the Canal: that there is practically nowhere to swim. I think this must count as the biggest single drawback to a canal holiday – certainly in the height of summer, when it can get very hot. Some of the rental boats tow behind them what look like enlarged paddling pools, which probably serve to quieten some of the younger ones, although I didn't like to imagine what the water might look like after a week. A couple of places had sports halls along the canal, but didn't advertise any swimming pools – either because they didn't think of it, or perhaps they didn't have one. I've suggested to the VNF that they produce a separate list of swimming pools close to the canal, although Crown Blue have one in their handbook. The alternative is to stay in the region around Cassefières, where the beaches and sea are within walking distance.

Gill phoned and told us that they were leaving and could get to the canal in half an hour. I checked our guide and told her that we'd meet them between PK74 and PK73. The silence which greeted this made me remember that she was looking at a different map. 'The name of the nearest village?' she asked.

I checked my guide. 'Pexiora,' I replied. 'There's a little road that seems to go down to the canal and then stop.'

'I should hope so,' Gill replied, I thought somewhat off the point.

'We'll be there in about twenty minutes,' I said confidently, but later, after we'd been waiting at the agreed spot for nearly fifteen minutes, the phone rang.

'Where are you?' It was Gill. 'We're here waiting for you.'

'No, you're not,' I replied testily.

'Yes, we are,' Gill was equally testy.

'If you're really here, then where are you?' I was aware that this wasn't the most instructive conversation. Eventually, by a laborious process of elimination, it emerged that there were several roads leading to the canal from Pexiora, but the one on our canal guide wasn't shown on their road map – and vice versa. We eventually identified one that was on both, and Gill was finally able to take Corinne off to the nearby *hypermarché*, while Ian continued with me. We optimistically agreed that we'd phone them later and let them know where we'd be. After all, we would only be going on a few kilometres; it couldn't be that difficult for them to find us again.

Of course we should have learnt by then that the perspective from the canal is utterly different from that of a car driver. Experienced denizens of the canals, amongst whom we now counted ourselves, see the rest of the world only as a piece of back-projection, having no real existence of its own. This view is reinforced by the Canal guides, which purvey a sort of solipsism by exaggerating the scale of the canal at the expense of the places around. To us the canal was broad, obvious and dominant. To the Michelin map it was a tiny and unimportant blue squiggle squeezed between the motorway, the mainline railway and the Route Nationale. To summarise, it was very difficult for them to find us again.

We couldn't see how they could miss us. The towpath was straight and wide enough to drive along without difficulty, and we could see that it joined the public road just half a kilometre ahead, so we tried to direct them towards it. What we couldn't see was the "No Entry" sign. It turned out that Corinne and Gill passed it several times but, unaccountably, took a no entry sign as a reason not to enter. I thought it showed rather a literal attitude to life and a more adventurous spirit would have explored further. That was before they told us that they'd nearly been recruited by the Foreign Legion instead – obviously an equal opportunities employer.

It turned out that the woods on the far side of the bank concealed a huge barracks, and they liked to keep their security tight. Gill had driven up what she thought was a promising little road leading to the canal, only to be stopped at a checkpoint by an armed guard who demanded to know what they were both doing trying to penetrate such an important military establishment. Of course Corinne's passport was on the boat and the more she tried to explain this, the less they believed her. They said that her French was just too good for an Englishwoman. That gave me a rare moment of pleasure when she told me about it later. Every time she opens her mouth in France I have to listen yet again to people telling her what wonderful French she speaks. I thought of the countless times I've to put up with people talking to me through her, as though dealing with a dim-witted child. Serves her right, I thought unkindly.

Eventually they identified the entrance to the towpath, and drove along the track towards us and unloaded the supplies. When we had finally stowed everything, it was almost dark and raining again. We were berthed between PK70 and PK69, just four kilometres from Castelnaudary, so Gill and Ian drove us in to look for the family hotel recommended by Gault Millaut and whose speciality was *cassoulet* – what else could it have been? Locals will tell you that the only *true* cassoulet comes from Castelnaudary – a huge dish of beans, ducks, pork, and garlic. In Toulouse they say it has to be made with local *saucisse*, while in Carcasonne it has to be mutton. An argument like this is taken very seriously in France. The writer Anatole France attempted reconciliation by saying that the *cassoulet* of Castelnaudary was God the Father, that of Carcasonne the Son, while Toulouse offered up the Holy Spirit. Such ethereal analogies seem completely inappropriate. Whichever version you choose, *cassoulet* is a substantial dish, perfect, perhaps for winter – but in summer? Even if it was raining…?

In Riquet's original route, the Canal didn't pass through Castelnaudary at all. It seems, as with Carcassonne, that this might have been a deliberate bluff, since as soon as the town council agreed to make a financial contribution, not only was the route quickly changed, but work started on the construction of a large basin in the very centre of town. This added not just to the commercial viability of the canal, but also contributed considerably to the prosperity of Castelnaudary itself, which became a major port central to the transport of wine and cereals from Lauragais. It soon became clear that although the lake was large enough to berth hundreds of barges, it offered little shelter, and in 1754 a large artificial island, L'Îsle de la Cybèle, was built to provide protection from the violent north-westerly winds. Later, as trade declined during the twentieth century, so did the town. Behind the attractive canal frontage the buildings are showing signs of considerable economic depression – although the boat-hire companies which have taken over from the commercial *peniches* still provide the town with some economic return from the Canal. I'm afraid I couldn't find much enthusiasm for Castelnaudary; perhaps that was only because it was raining, but we decided that the main attraction of the canals lies in the countryside and small villages, and the cities were best left for another time.

Chapter Five

*Irrigation canal bringing water from reservoirs in the Montagne Noir to
the watershed at the Seuil de Narouze*

Enclosed in a tunnel of trees, the Canal seems to exist in a world of
its own, an independent community of boaters, fishermen, cyclists,
walkers and joggers. Set apart from most of the villages it passes, the
bridges carried only tiny country lanes which seemed to link nothing
to nowhere. Even the mainline railway and the motorway which
shadowed us intruded only occasionally. All activity was centred
around the water and its towpath, giving a feeling that we were all

members of a private club, greeting each other on passing as though we shared a common secret.

But it is in the locks that the true atmosphere of a canal is to be found. There's the keeper to chat to, often students anxious to practise their English, and an incredible variety of people of diverse nationalities and languages. The inhabitants of this Provençal Babel were not only on other boats, but on the towpaths and bridges, or just watching the action at the locks. Each stretch seems to develop its own unique rhythm – boats bunch together and often spend an entire day travelling in convoy. Over the days, small communities continually form and reform as people delay or go on ahead. Sometimes people catch up with you several days later, while others take the passage so slowly that they are still there even after several years.

The locks on the Canal du Midi seem to be more reliable than the later ones on the Canal Latéral. Perhaps this is because only a few locks are fully "automatisée" and so there's less to go wrong. A "mechanic" lock means the gates and sluices use separate electric motors to power the worm-drives of each, and both are operated by the lock-keeper from an adjacent control box. But more than half are described as "manual", which generally means that although the gates themselves are powered, the sluices still have to be worked by hand and the lock-keeper has to keep going backwards and forwards between the controls by each set of gates. Inevitably he was in the wrong place when, as were leaving one lock, the gates started to shut on us, apparently entirely of their own accord.

Corinne yelled at the lock-keeper, but the boat was already moving. I had to make an instant decision: full astern or full ahead. Either I could try to stop the boat before it reached the gates, or I could accelerate, hoping to pass through before they shut. Whatever I decided, if I got it wrong, *Calypso* was going to be squashed. It probably suggests something about my character that I pushed the throttle lever full open – ahead. After that the adrenalin was surging and everything slowed down. Why couldn't the boat accelerate faster?

Why couldn't the gates move more slowly? Why couldn't the lock-keeper run faster? He was making good time, but was still only halfway to the emergency button and the bows were already abreast of the closing gates. I couldn't tell if we were going to make it.

There was nothing more to be said or done. Corinne and I just stared at the gates – we were going quite fast now and if we could get halfway through, then as the hull narrowed towards the stern, we might gain a few valuable seconds. It's always difficult to gauge distances accurately on a boat. Like watching an approaching ship at sea when trying to work out whether you're on a collision course, there's a moment when it abruptly "clicks" and you suddenly see whether or not you're going to make it. It clicked – and we weren't.

I think the lock-keeper felt that his honour was at stake – a yacht impaled on his lock doors would not look good on his escutcheon. Whatever it was that was motivated him, his leap was heroic. As was his aim. He caught the red button with the tips of his fingers and the mechanism stopped immediately. We surged between the doors with just a few inches to spare on either side.

The reaches immediately upstream of Castelnaudary are especially attractive. The locks come and go and there is an atmosphere of ease and contentment. We were now approaching the watershed at Naurouze and, in terms of locks if not distance, were almost halfway to Bordeaux. We slowly realised that we were we now feeling completely at home and had started taking it for granted that we were going to make it to the end.

We reached the Seuil de Naurouze on our sixth day. The narrow irrigation canal, which joined the main canal on the *bief de partage des eaux*, gave little indication of the huge reservoirs behind it. Knowing of the breakthrough Riquet had made in harnessing the mountain waters, it felt almost an anticlimax. This top stretch was originally intended to be a large basin that would also act as a reservoir. Unfortunately all the mud and sediment brought down from the mountains meant that it kept silting up. In 1686 Vauban decided to short-circuit this stretch entirely by digging a new canal which would not only bypass the basin, but also the two locks on either side of the *partage*. Since it was considered important to retain the evocative names of *L'Océan* and *Méditerranée*, the next two locks, formerly called *Montferrand* and *Medécin*, were simply renamed.

The remains of the original works are still there, and there's a tourist trail which passes through the old arboretum leading to the remains of old Mediterranean lock. Further on, *l'ouvrage d'alimentation* controls the 30 million cubic metres of water which enter the canal each year. This is the highest point of the canal at 189.43 metres, and from here the water supplied to the Canal is controlled, depending upon usage. This used to be done manually through *l'épanchoir de Narouze*, but an automatic system has now replaced it.

The old basin, surrounded by an alley of 200-year-old plane trees, was almost literally carved out of the hard rock of which Naurouze mainly consists. Indeed its hardness was always considered one of the major obstacles to the construction of a canal. Riquet wanted to turn it to his advantage and originally planned the construction of a major canal settlement, complete with a church, arsenal and shops, but only the *Maison de l'ingénieur du Canal* was ever built. This building, alongside the tourist office, was where Maréchal Soult and the Duke of Welling-ton signed the armistice on 18th April 1814. Past this, an obelisk erected by Riquet's family in 1827 commemorates their ancestor's unique achievements.

It was literally downhill from here and the locks suddenly became much easier. Instead of water cascading in, it emptied from the locks and caused little turbulence. It was also much easier to moor the boat since we no longer faced the inside of a blank wall and had to throw the lines up; we were now looking down on the quay and became practised in lassoing the bollards. Indeed, I even managed to go through a dozen locks single-handed when Corinne returned to

London for a few days, and I found it a relatively simply matter to stand at the centre of the boat letting out the fore and aft lines as the boat sank in the lock.

The watershed had the geographical effect of funnelling all routes close together, and for the stretch into Toulouse the canal was now joined by the A61 motorway, as well as the mainline railway. The first sign of this, ironically, was the vast *halte nautique* immediately after Naurouse at Port Lauragais (PK50). Having almost forgotten about the outside world, it was a shock to find that this huge basin shares its facilities with the motorway service station. Although the economic rationale is obvious, I am surprised that anyone would want to stay here. It's extremely well kept and well equipped, there's plenty of room for boats and they've certainly done their best with the landscaping. I admire their efforts, but at the end of the day (figuratively and metaphorically) it will always be a motorway service station.

Of course you never know what people will like, but a few hours here is a different matter. The *Centre Pierre-Paul Riquet* is a worthy effort at outlining some of the history of the canal and has a range of historic documents and plans on show. Oh, and there's a rugby museum as well: the *Musée de l'Ovalie*. The entire complex is the sort of *grand projet* that the French love to build and visit, but whether others have an equal enthusiasm for it is another matter. I can understand that boats must be a draw for the motorists, but since cars are unlikely ever to be an attraction for boaters, it seems rather a one-sided arrangement.

Renneville (PK43) has a pretty quay, but we were aiming for a bend in the Canal further on at around PK40, which looked as though it would be reasonably protected from the motorway and railway. The map shows these as running almost side by side, but in fact for most of the time we remained unaware of them. We moored for the night with good views across the surrounding fields and found it tranquil, in spite of another stormy night.

It was still wet and cold when we arrived the next day at Encassan (PK46). When they first filled the lock in 1672, it was immediately clear that something had gone wrong when the fall turned out to be much higher than they expected, forcing them to build a second chamber quickly. Further on, the Negra lock was the first overnight stop for the *barque de poste* from Toulouse and the complex of build-ings contained not just the *hostellerie*, but a chapel, stables and even an icehouse. It was here that we saw our first New Zealand flag. We had caught up with a very smart, well-maintained Dutch steel motor boat, but the Union flag on the elaborate blue ensign was unmistakeable and I could only assume that the owner was a member of New Zealand's equivalent to the Royal Yacht Squadron. There was a low bridge just in front of the lock, and as the lock gates opened to let us in, the skipper lowered the flagstaff before passing under it. I was taken aback – it seemed so disrespectful to such a magnificent ensign. 'Aren't you supposed to salute it before you take it down?' I asked facetiously as we waited together inside the lock.

'No,' he replied without hesitation. 'You are.'

The Canal is always at its most attractive when it passes through a village. Then, as at Renneville, with its appealing waterfront and shady lock, the two seem to complement each other and create more than the sum of the parts. The canal's interaction with the communities it passes through has not always been simply a matter of transport. The local farmers have been pumping out water under licence from the Canal authorities for centuries, and the fifth reservoir in the Pyrénées now offers them a much more reliable supply. Water wasn't just taken for irrigation, but also for washing. Just outside the lock at Montgis-card is a delightful old *laverie* that dates back to the very first days of the canal. (There's another one by the Colombiers lock near Montady.)

But we were now nearing the end. For the past week we had looked ahead at this last stretch of the Canal du Midi as the real test of our passage. We'd been told by a keel-boat that the stretch just above Toulouse was very shallow and that they had kept hitting tree roots. If it was worse than the reach just below Carcassonne, then we knew we would be facing some real problems. I was therefore going slowly and carefully as we approached Toulouse and didn't have much time to take in the surroundings, which had become increasingly built-up and industrial. Both Corinne and I couldn't shake off the feeling that the canal we had come to know was disappearing behind us.

We had been given an enthusiastic review of Port Sud by an English family we had met earlier on the Canal. They had told us what a lovely place it was, saying that they'd stayed for nearly a week, and we were hopeful that it would make a better stop than in the centre of the city. In the event it turned out to be quite appalling: half a dozen hideous pink apartment blocks surrounding a nondescript basin. It was a sort of scaled-down version of one of the horrendous marina nightmares in which the French specialise. (Some of their monumental skiing resorts are unbelievably ugly as well – making me wonder why they deliberately turn their backs on their enviable rural heritage and tradition. So many of their modern architectural efforts are like sticking a fluorescent patch on a comfortable pair of trousers.) Before leaving for the city centre we took advantage of their fuel quay and filled up with diesel. Well, not filled up. They don't take credit cards and we didn't have enough cash for a full tank. France is a country that accepts credit cards almost everywhere, and I have no idea why, if you need fuel on the Canals, you need cash. The only other place I've ever come across with a similar attitude is Antibes, where the overnight cost for the relatively diminutive *Calypso* must mean that a super-yacht would need a wheelbarrow to carry the banknotes to the *Capitainerie*.

In spite of all the earlier dire warnings, we got through to the city centre without any problems – perhaps the torrents of rain we had endured had raised the levels. But at Port St Saveur, the municipal pontoons in the centre of the city, the water was very shallow. Sylvie, the dockmaster (although judging by her affection for the place, dockmistress would be a more appropriate term), was solicitous in finding us a berth with enough depth, and we eventually tied up outside a welcoming Dutch steel canal boat. This one had real Dutchmen on board who were very amiable, in spite of just having had one of their very expensive folding bicycles stolen. For some reason many yachtsmen seem to regard themselves as immune from crime, and if they become victims of it find it almost impossible to understand why anyone should target *them* – as if a dinghy and outboard left alongside a quay in the centre of a run-down southern Italian city wouldn't be a temptation to someone with no money. Our Dutch neighbours took it all very philosophically, recognising that these things happen in the centre of any large city, and they were annoyed more at the inconvenience than the crime.

In geographical terms, we were now halfway. Both Sète and Bordeaux are roughly the same distance from Toulouse, about 240 kms. In terms of time, however, from Port St. Saveur there were now only four locks to the end of the Canal du Midi and another 53 locks, all single basin, on the Canal Latéral. We had already been through 59 locks with nearly 90 separate basins. So although only halfway by distance, we estimated that we were probably nearer two-thirds of the way in time. And this proved to be roughly correct. Excluding our day off in Carcassonne, we had been travelling for seven days since leaving the Étang de Thau – three days more than the *barque de poste*. I thought that we needed another four to get to the end of the canal at Castets-en-Dorthe. I sat down and filled in the log with something that a few months earlier, I'd never dreamt I'd write.

"Moored Toulouse."

Above: the central canal in Sète
Below: oyster beds in the Étang de Thau

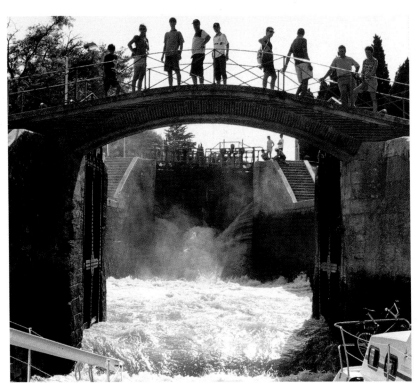

Above and below: the locks of Fonsérannes

Above: evening up-river of Béziers
Below: the 13th-century Étang de Montady

Above: a rare straight reach on the Canal du Midi
Below: giving way to a barge

Above: towers of the medieval Cité of Carcassonne
Below: characteristic olive-shaped lock in deep countryside

Above: Sunday market at St Aubin, Toulouse
Below: the boat basin at Montech

Above: the Pente d'Eau (water slope) at Montech
Below: the viaduct over the Tarn River at Agen

Above: Sunday lunch near Lagruère
Below: using the tender to get ashore

Chapter Six

Although now in the centre of a major city and apparently far from the pastoral reaches of the old Canal, Sylvie re-established our link with the Canal's past. Her family had worked the barges for countless generations and she had lived on the Canal since she was born. When commercial traffic ended she and her family found themselves unable to adapt to life ashore and eventually moved back onto a boat on a permanent mooring. Her husband had also worked the barges, but after a few unhappy years as a lorry driver, he had taken a lower-paid job as deck hand on one of the *peniches* carrying tourists on the Garonne. The canal was in their blood – even their daughter was a lock keeper. Sylvie understood the problems of deeper-draught boats and later told us that when she was a girl the old barges couldn't moor alongside the banks either. 'The boats had a wooden bar hinged at the bows. You had to lean over it and kick to make it swing out over the towpath.' She laughed. 'Sometimes, if we didn't push hard enough, it stopped halfway and we'd have to drop into the water and swim to the bank.'

The new *Capitainerie* at Port St Saveur has impressive facilities: showers, washing machines, even a fuel quay. There's an adjacent VNF agency which also doubles up as a tourist office. Sylvia had recently been confirmed as its permanent "harbourmaster" and was determined to turn it into a place that boats couldn't leave out of their itinerary. 'I'm not going to let it fill up with lots of old local boats that are never used,' she told me. 'There are too many ports where there's no room left for visitors. I'm not going to let that happen here.' Given our experiences in ports throughout the Mediterranean, I agreed with her completely. I thought of Cetara, near Salerno, and wondered again how long it would be before it was full. The phenomenon had also been noticeable on the canals. When the *halte nautique* is owned by the council, they'll generally favour local boats which don't usually pay an economic rate for their berths. As a result, just like so many marinas, many of the *bassins* fill up with a range of dilapidated boats which were rarely, if ever, used. I remember waiting to speak to the harbourmaster of Villefranche marina, which is owned by the commune of Nice. The man in front of me, who was carrying a little boy on his shoulders, was asking how much longer he would have to wait for a permanent berth. 'How long have you been on the waiting list?' the harbourmaster asked.

'It's over seven years now,' the man replied, with a hint of pride.

The harbourmaster shrugged, and then looked up at the little boy. 'I think you might get it in time for *him*,' he said.

To be fair to Villefranche and to Nice, they operate a policy of always finding space for visiting boats, however full they are. The alternative, I suppose, is to let the market decide and keep putting up prices until there's no waiting list – they're attempting this along the coast in Cannes, where berth-holders have started legal action to fight attempts to price them out. It's like the operators of marinas in the south coast of England who think that if there's a waiting list, they can't be charging enough.

We hadn't planned to spend any time in Toulouse. Apart from having to get *Calypso* home on time, I have already recorded that we find it difficult to mix the rural with the urban, and a big city simply doesn't appeal. Instead we decided to do some research and started swapping notes with the numerous boats moored in St Saveur. Incredibly we heard yet again from one English boat that we'd never make it to Bordeaux. This time we knew better, and we just ignored the advice.

Before it got dark we decided to take a short stroll around the streets. Expecting the wide, almost unmanageable thoroughfares of a major city we were amazed to discover that this part of Toulouse at least, was more like a large village. A network of apparently random streets of charming brick houses made it feel almost cosy. Each house was different from its neighbours and I felt ashamed that I had so thoughtlessly prejudged it. I will return.

On the next day, a Sunday, there was an important street market around the St Aubin church, very close to the Canal. Sylvie said we couldn't possibly miss it and Corinne needs little – make that no – encouragement to visit any street market, anywhere. While she was investigating, I took another look at the neighbourhood. French cities always seem to look their best early on a Sunday morning. There is something intimate about the way the neighbourhoods wake up slowly, sending out drowsy scouts along the streets as though to check for signs of life: to the bakers, or to get a paper, stopping to get a *grande crème* at a pavement café. I felt a bit like a voyeur intruding into a private world.

The market is absolutely magnificent. A classic. Essentially a farmer's market it has every type of agricultural product, both dead and alive. I was very taken by a rabbit that looked at me with melting eyes. Corinne, heartlessly told me not to be so silly. I expected to see Brigette Bardot turn up any moment and buy the lot of them to save them from the pot.

Now fully provisioned, we set off for the new lock in the centre of the city, directly opposite the railway station. It's been converted from a double to a single and has a fall of over 6 metres. The lock keeper – Sylvie's daughter-in-law – photographed us with our camera as she lowered us towards the Canal's rather ignominious end. Two locks further on, Riquet's 320-year-old canal peters out in an anonymous pool with not even a signpost to mark it. Absolutely nothing. Not even a milestone. We really felt for the old boy. One of Béziers' favourite sons and the grand folk of Toulouse couldn't be bothered even to put up a sign.

The original Port de l'Embouchure was built in 1670 and originally provided the link between the Canal du Midi and the Garonne River, through the Canal de Brienne, but it was substantially enlarged in both the subsequent centuries – the marble bas-relief between the original "Twin Bridges" was sculpted in 1775. (The bridges were later the scene of bloody fighting between Wellington and Maréchal Soult in 1814.) With the construction of the Canal Latéral, the third arch was added in 1843.

The Port de l'Embouchure is big. Once we had entered from the last bridge of the Canal du Midi it wasn't at all clear where we should go, so we carried straight on until we realised it was a cul-de-sac. Turning around and going back, all we could see were three apparently identical bridges over three waterways leading in different directions. Not only could we not tell where we should go, we couldn't even tell where we had come from. Uncertainly we decided to turn left, but stopped alongside a nearby barge and asked the woman on board whether this was the Canal Latérale. I felt a complete idiot, although slightly less so when she said she didn't know either and that she had to ask her boyfriend. It was, and we continued on our way.

The Canal Latérale à la Garonne has a very different character. Passing through the industrial suburbs and marshalling yards of Toulouse, the magnificent circling silhouettes of the buzzards preying on the rodents inhabiting the railway tracks was a frequent sight. But although it felt harsh, the canal was well-tended and clean. Eventually the landscape softened and we were back in the countryside, which was much less populated than the Canal du Midi, and fruit orchards now replaced the vineyards of the Languedoc. The landscape is flatter and somehow felt more bland – the reaches are straighter and the locks are no longer the familiar oval shape.

In fact many of the locks near Toulouse are almost literally soulless. Most are automatic – there is no lock keeper and a boat has to stop and twist a control wire hanging above the canal some 200m before the lock. Immediately after twisting the cable, if there's nothing coming in the opposite direction, the traffic lights change to amber and a boat should approach the lock to wait for the gates to open. Once moored inside, we found the control panel was on the upstream side and we had to cross the downstream lock gates to reach the green button that started the cycle, and then sprint back just in case anything went wrong. A piece of cake. We passed through the first half a dozen locks quite happily until, arriving at the next one, however much we twisted the cable, the lights refused to change and the lock gates stayed shut. This was complicated by the fact that there was by now a considerable cross-wind and the flat land around us provided no shelter. Trying to hold our position was almost impossible. We approached the closed doors of the lock. Next to the green button on the control panel was a sort of entryphone arrangement, connected directly to the regional office. We decided that I'd better try to put

Corinne ashore so that she could call them. Simple, you would have thought.

Actually it was quite impossible. The water was too shallow to get alongside the bank, and even if it hadn't been, the freshening wind was making it difficult to manoeuvre. If I wasn't careful we'd be blown across the canal and get stuck in the mud without any way of getting off. It suddenly occurred to me that we had a problem. Not only could Corinne not get ashore, but I'd have to continue motoring up and down the canal until somehow we could get the lock gates open. I realised we'd have to anchor.

Anchoring in two metres of water? It seemed so unlikely, but I couldn't think of an alternative. The canal was only slightly wider than the length of our boat and we'd be straddling the canal like a stopper in a bottle. I turned into wind and Corinne dropped the anchor as the bows nudged the mud on one side. We fell back on the chain until the rudder nudged the mud on the other side. When I was sure the anchor was holding I sat down in the cockpit and considered our position. I felt a complete prat.

'Lunch?' asked Corinne cheerfully. I nodded glumly. She went below and I set up the table. As she passed up the dishes, I had a thought.

'You don't think...' I stopped and looked at her. She was obviously thinking the same thing. 'It's not possible, is it?'

'We *are* in France,' she replied thoughtfully.

Of course! We were looking at it with an Anglo-Saxon logic, entirely alien to the Gallic. However much I honour and revere the French attitude to meals, it simply hadn't occurred to us that when they built an automatic lock, they programme it to shut down for lunch. When we'd finished ours, we pulled up the anchor and returned to the control wire. Twisting it, the traffic lights immediately turned amber and the lock started to fill. Silly us.

But of course that didn't mean that the lock was working properly. Having moored up inside and gone on shore to push the green button, the gates refused to shut. I called up the control centre on the entryphone. It seems there's a beam you pass through on entering the lock which tells the machinery that a boat is waiting in the lock. Somehow it hadn't been triggered as we had entered. I was told to lean over and look for it somewhere near the gates and cover it with my hand. I did, and this time heard a reassuring clunk from the machinery box. When I pressed the button again, the gates immediately started to close. But I wasn't quite done, and called up the control room and asked for their landline number. Next time if we couldn't get in, at least we could phone up on the mobile.

According to the guide, we should reach the Forêt de Montech by the evening and it seemed quite promising. From our experiences on the Canal du Midi, I wasn't expecting much from Montech itself, lying just beyond the lock, but Corinne had to leave the next day to fly back to London to be with our daughter when she received her A-level exam results, so a night alone in the deep countryside seemed appropriate. After a quiet night we left the next day and passed through the lock into the small, but immaculately kept *halte nautique* at Montech. The office claims to be manned every day of the year which, when you consider the berthing fee is around €3 a night, is extraordinarily generous of the local commune. Given how few boats there were, even in high season, the harbour master's job must be for someone who's got very behind with their reading.

Montech's sole taxi driver took Corinne off to Toulouse airport, and I strolled into the town to find that I had been completely wrong about it: it was quite perfect. At its centre was a little grid of cobbled streets leading to a magnificent church. Next to this was the town square, which even had a small street market. But apart from that, what more can you ask for from a town when you intend to stay a few days peacefully writing? It had one hotel/restaurant, two bars and three *boulangeries.*

When I emerged blearily from the cabin next morning to inspect the day, I did a rapid double take as a lion crossed the bridge. Yes, it was a lion. Not only that but a couple of tigers followed it on the back of a lorry. My sleepy brain slowly worked out that The Circus Was In Town! Later that afternoon I strolled along the canal where two camels, some llamas and a Shetland pony seemed quite at home grazing peacefully on the towpath.

The atmosphere was so much more low-key than further south. This was a sleepy place – the only action was the occasional convoy of Portuguese-registered camper vans which toured the area in season as itinerant fruit pickers. Few boats passed until I saw the New Zealand boat we had passed earlier arrive and moor next to me. We nodded cordially at one another but later that evening, when I was still trying to decide whether to go off to the circus, her skipper emerged on deck wearing a beret and carrying a set of bagpipes. Once he had embarked on an irredeemably forlorn (and very loud) recital – I made up my mind instantly and fled.

It was a tiny circus, the members being apparently Portuguese Romanies – the snake charmer-cum-usher had the most magnificently swarthy hooked nose, reminiscent of an aerial view of the Rocky Mountains. But although I don't usually worry about these things, I had to recognise that their show was everything politically incorrect and then some. Even the animals seemed slightly apologetic that they were being forced to go through a routine so irredeemably old-hat. When a three-year-old girl came on and started gyrating with an increasing number of hula-hoops, I couldn't stand any more and left hoping that no one noticed. Since I was the only single, middle-aged person in the ringside seats, I don't supposed they cared. Fortunately when I got back the piper seemed to have retired for the night and the quay was quiet. The next morning when he came over for a chat, I thought I showed the most amazing restraint by not reminding him of the Irish definition of a gentleman as someone who knows how to play the pipes, but doesn't.

Montech's main claim to fame, however, is the nearby *Pente d'Eau*, or water slope, an alternative to a series of five locks on the main canal. A giant plunger is held between two huge locomotives which run it through a sloping concrete trough more than a kilometre long. The plunger holds back enough water for a barge to float in, and then pushes it up or down the slope. It's an extraordinary contraption and I was dying to try it out, but unfortunately they wouldn't let keel-boats through.

I passed a quiet few days until Corinne was due to come back. While waiting at the airport on her way out, she'd discovered that the next town along, Castelsarrasin, was on the main railway line from Toulouse. I reluctantly agreed to meet her there, and left peaceful Montech with regret – although it was unlikely to remain so quiet since a three-day *boules* championship was due to start the next day. Immediately downstream, adjacent to the *pente d'eau*, an arm of the canal branches off to Montauban, which is the major tourist attraction of the region. Although it hadn't been used for years, they're working on reopening it sometime in 2003. I went on regretfully through the next five locks, looking wistfully across to the adjacent *pente d'eau* which seemed more like a funfair ride than a genuine method of transport. Perhaps they should link up with the circus.

Unlike the Canal du Midi, where each lock has its own keeper, locks on the Canal Latéral are often grouped together, with just one lock-keeper riding between the them on a motocyclette. Such was the case with these five Peyrets locks, which I fortunately managed to get through without difficulty. It was a student stand-in and by the time I left the last lock, we had become quite chummy.

It was only 13 km to Castelsarrasin, and although the Port Jaques-Yves Cousteau at its centre is extremely well equipped, I found the place rather bland. It was too big to have the attraction of Montech, although I did manage to find a surprisingly good restaurant where I took Corinne for a late lunch when she finally arrived from the airport.

We decided not to stay, and set off that afternoon for Moissac, just 8 km downstream. Leaving the town, the canal follows the hillside on the edge of the valley, presumably to avoid the flooding of the River

Tarn which now runs alongside before it reaches the Garonne. I thought that there should be a good stopping place overlooking the river at the Petit Bézy lock at PK 71. The railway, although very close, was almost hidden in the trees, and we soon became accustomed to the bells ringing on the nearby level crossing.

Corinne was back on board. Carla had done excellently in her exams. All was well with the world.

Chapter Seven

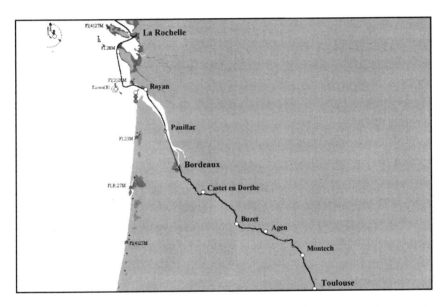

After my few days off in Montech, it felt almost like going back to work after a holiday – boating is often at its most perfect when you're doing nothing and going nowhere. But I was anxious not to lose time, partly because I wasn't sure how easy it would be to find somewhere to restep the mast, and partly because if we were delayed by bad weather in Brittany, we'd miss our haul-out deadline in Lymington. But it was a frustrating morning, dogged by a succession of broken-down locks. Not for the first time our mobile phone proved invaluable, allowing us to call the local maintenance offices for help. We learnt always to find the number of the next VNF office when entering a lock.

After Agen, known as much for its rugby as its superb prunes, we crossed the magnificent aqueduct above the Garonne and re-entered the wine-growing area – the suburbs, if you like, of the Bordeaux vineyards. The area to the south and west is where Armagnac comes from, and the capital of the region is the aptly named town of Buzet. Approaching it, the Canal is almost completely surrounded by vineyards, and the towpath was lined with advertisements for *dégustation* of their products. The canal was now much more varied; there were more people about and more facilities. Further back, towards Toulouse, many of the communes had made half-hearted attempts at building a local *halte nautique* to encourage visitors, but most had withered through lack of use. Now they were becoming much more popular and, perhaps because we were getting closer to Bordeaux, there were many more private boats. Overall, the canal was becoming increasingly lively – the busy little basin in Buzet even had a guitarist playing outside the waterside café/restaurant. We had a drink there with a couple from Bordeaux who keep their own boat on the canal and spend a couple of months pottering around on it every year. The fact that he was a retired *vignobleron* (if that's the right word – he sold vines rather than grew them) added verisimilitude to the local atmosphere.

Before leaving the next morning we wandered up into the town and bought some local produce from the little shop – I've since become quite hooked on the Buzet *appellations*. It was Sunday; the town was quiet and the *dégustations* were closed, so after a quick look around we went back down to the boat and set off on what was to be our last full day on the Canal. Just before the village of Lagruère (PK153) we passed several people sitting at tables outside a small restaurant on the bank and, like a double take in slow motion, I continued for some distance before realising that Sunday lunch by the canal was an opportunity too good to miss. We managed a three-point turn (with a little help from the bow-thruster) and went back and moored alongside – on our last day I had finally learnt to seize the opportunity when it came.

Later, relaxing with our hors d'oeuvres and a bottle of wine in front of us, a man at the next table asked us where we'd come from. When we told him the Mediterranean, he looked across at *Calypso* with a puzzled expression. After thinking for a moment or two, he turned back to us and said, 'But you're going the wrong way.'

That evening we arrived at the end of the Canal, at its junction with the navigable Garonne River in Castets-en-Dorthe. Since leaving Toulouse we had travelled 193 km through 53 locks. Bordeaux was 54 km ahead of us and Royan, at the entrance to the Gironde, another 100 km. The Mediterranean was now just a memory and we were back in tidal waters. There is an extraordinary range even this far (54 km) up-river of Bordeaux, which is further aggravated by frequent flooding. The lock-keeper's house is the only three-story lock house on the Canal, and had an enormous tide gauge fixed on its front to mark the levels of the flood-water in previous years. The highest mark reached the second floor, twenty-five feet up.

That evening I sat down with tide tables for the first time in four years. I was anxious that I would have forgotten how to work out a tidal plan this far up-river, but it soon came back to me – even the computer screen was now happily showing the tidal currents out at sea, something it hadn't been required to do in the Mediterranean. To carry the ebb through to Bordeaux, I calculated that the current would be with us from early the next morning, but when we tried to leave at nine the following day, we found the lock gates were closed fast. I found the lock-keeper (another student), who rather sheepishly told me he'd lost the key; he also told me that it wasn't the right time to leave anyway, because the tide was wrong. While he went off to get help from the VNF regional office, I checked and double-checked the tidal information, but still thought we should leave as soon as we could. When he returned I showed him my calculations, but it made no difference. They have a rigid, if simplistic, rule that boats must leave for Bordeaux at high water and only at high water, as though the flood and ebb each last six hours and remain the same whether it's a spring or neap tide. To be fair, we had heard that there are regular groundings in the upper reaches, sometimes with disastrous consequences, and so in the end I gave up arguing and we decided instead to pass the time with a leisurely lunch at the restaurant nearby on the towpath, and leave later in the afternoon as suggested. They have a reputation for their eel – a local speciality, and it's well worth trying – cooked in oil with herbs and copious amounts of garlic.

It was here that we finally met André Fromilhague. I'd phoned him a few days earlier to tell him of our progress and he'd worked out that we'd probably be in Castets and telephoned the lock-keeper. He had obviously been given a somewhat embellished account of my attempts to leave before I was supposed to, and drove down from Bordeaux to find out what the trouble was. I told him that, as always, I was doing what I was told and he seemed reassured in spite of Corinne's involuntary snort. Over a coffee in the cockpit, he told us that he'd made arrangements for us to stay at a boatyard on the right bank of the river, just by the Pont de Pierre in the centre of Bordeaux. He explained that the alternative was the *bassin à flot* further downstream, but he said it was in a very run-down part of the city. Apart from staying in an area with little to recommend it, the idea of locking in didn't appeal since it would restrict on our access to a favourable tide the next morning. André also told us that he'd made arrangements with the port office in Pauillac to step our mast and so we agreed to meet him there in a couple of days.

The student had by now found the key and lowered us through the lock and into the river. There was now nothing between us and the South Coast of England, except a great deal of water.

The passage along the lower Garonne is dramatic, almost harsh, despite the flowing vineyards carpeting the hills nearby. This is the home of sweet whites; the small towns of Cadillac and Barsac reach down to the banks, while Yquem and Sauternes are only a few kilometres away. We were swept past the dozens of magnificent châteaux overlooking the river, with hardly time to admire them. Along the entire length of the river bank were fishing huts, often built on rickety, stilted pontoons far above the normal high-tide level, where fishermen sat by large framed nets, like spiders watching over their webs. But the sky was becoming overcast and it was getting prematurely gloomy. I didn't fancy travelling in the dark and decided to abandon our attempt to make Bordeaux that evening. Instead we started to look out for places to stop, but the current was carrying us along so fast that it was obvious that we wouldn't be able to moor alongside the bank, even if there was enough water. There were virtually no public moorings marked and the few that we passed were isolated and unwelcoming.

Nearly three hours after leaving Castets we finally came across an empty pontoon alongside the small village of Langoiran, halfway to Bordeaux. It looked perfect and we turned to face the fierce current, only to be swept several hundred yards downstream before managing to crab our way back. When we were finally secured alongside the pontoon I must have put out over half a dozen mooring lines, but still remained anxious. Like most things that appear alarming, unfamiliarity had a lot to do with it. Two youngsters on a dinghy were tacking back towards the pontoon, but with so little wind I didn't give much for their chances of being able to turn against the current. I stopped trying to fix yet another mooring line and ran to help them as they approached. A lucky grab caught a shroud and I managed to heave them back before their boat was swept under our bows. I thought they'd been incredibly lucky, but neither of them seemed remotely concerned as they hopped nonchalantly ashore. They still needed some help to pull the dinghy onto the pontoon – it was half full of water. As they packed their gear, a woman, obviously their mother, came down the gangway to meet them and while waiting for them to finish she started chatting to us. I was surprised at how little concern she seemed to show for the dangers her two sons might be facing, and suggested tentatively that it might be an idea if they wore lifejackets. 'But they always do!' she replied confidently. Corinne and I looked at one another, deciding whether or not to disabuse her. Instead we glanced across to where the boys were collecting their things with not a lifejacket in sight. The woman said something under her breath, clearly intending to deal with them later.

I suppose they had become quite used to the strength of the current, which didn't seem to hold the same fear for them. But then she told us that the pontoon had only just been replaced, having been destroyed the previous year when an unmanned barge worked free from its moorings and smashed into it. She said they'd heard the crash from their house nearly half a kilometre away. As though mention of her nearby house showed a lack of hospitality, she then invited us up for an aperitif, but I couldn't bear the thought of leaving poor *Calypso* to the mercy of such an apparently dangerous river, and we declined regretfully.

The image of several hundred tons of out-of-control barge careering downstream at anything up to five knots did nothing to help our sleep that night. A fierce thunderstorm added a gothic feeling of impending doom and when a splintering crash woke us at about three o'clock in the morning, we rushed on deck convinced we had only a few seconds to live. But although we inspected the boat carefully, we could see no sign of damage, nor of what had caused the impact. Just as we were going back below I noticed the looming outline of a commercial barge thundering along in the middle of the river. As it passed I could just make out its navigation lights, faint in the driving rain. I shivered slightly and slept very badly.

It was only in the morning that we saw that what looked like half a tree had rammed the piles and was now trapped underneath the pontoon with the current tearing at its branches. Random logs are a well-known problem in the estuary but I had tended to discount them, assuming that they would at least be visible. It hadn't occurred to me that they would attack at night, but the danger is obviously taken very seriously. Later, in Royan, we watched as a lifeboat came in with its blue light flashing. Towed behind, on a short rope, was a huge log which would scarcely have been visible at all had it not been for the diver sitting astride it.

Once again my tidal calculations indicated that if we left early we would have almost the entire ebb tide at our disposal, and this was simply too good an opportunity to turn up. Before leaving we had the rare luxury of a proper continental breakfast, with a choice of *boulangeries* in the centre of this pretty little town. I reckoned that we should even be able to make it in one leg to Pauillac, and so we reluctantly decided not to stop at Bordeaux (yet another city to return to).

The lower reaches of the Garonne, as well as the Gironde itself, can be navigated by a yacht only with a favourable tide; fighting against the current would be a waste of time. We swept under the Pont de Pierre at Bordeaux with our GPS showing over 12 knots as we left the city centre and continued past the straggling outskirts of wharfs and dockyard. The grey/brown industrial landscape, like a Lowry painting, appeared flat with little perspective in the hazy light.

Bordeaux comes to an enforced end in the peninsula of the Bec d'Ambes and we were back in wine country. The Dordogne river joins here, passing the low, serene hills of Côtes de Bourg and reminiscent of a country cousin coming up to town, happily unaware of the rough times ahead. The muddy river, now reborn as La Gironde, broadened until the far bank was almost invisible. In places the fierce current made the dark water boil, more drinking chocolate than weak tea. To our left, on the south bank, was the start of the Médoc, but the landscape was flat and unprepossessing, hardly appearing worthy of the great names it contained: Margaux, Beycheville, Mouton Rothschild, and finally our destination: Pauillac.

There are no natural harbours in the Gironde until it joins the sea near Royan. The rather grim marina at Pauillac is formed by a steel enclosure of sheet piling which is not enough to keep out the scouring tidal currents and at low tide many of the boats settle into the mud, while the entrance is inaccessible to anything other than dinghies. We moored on the waiting pontoon in the channel and set off to see a man about a crane. André Fromilhague had warned the port office of our arrival and we were assured by the young port manager that his staff would return after lunch. He pointed out the fixed crane on the quayside which was high and dry amid the dark red mud, and told us that we would be able to get alongside shortly after three o'clock. This was the moment I had been worrying about for months, and I spent an anxious three hours wandering around the town trying to put the question out of my mind: would we get everything connected again?

The crane operator and his assistant arrived punctually, a cheerful couple who, judging by their non-stop chatter, were obviously used to working together. With the crane's hook attached only slightly higher than the mast's centre of gravity, it was a relatively easy matter to guide its base into the stepping plate. Then out with the bottle screws to attach the inner and then the cap shrouds. André turned up to lend a hand and I left them to fix the fore and back stays, while I threaded the cables through the deck glands, took a deep breath and went below to connect them. A couple of hours later it was all done. I fired up the radar, watching the display nervously as it slowly came back to life. The anxiety of the past months fell away as the steel wall of the marina pilings emerged as a green, solid ring on the screen. We were done. Corinne set off to the tourist office to collect our trophy – a complimentary bottle of wine from a local Pauillac co-operative.

In contrast to its wines, the town itself is regrettably unprepossessing. The tidal range on the muddy foreshore means the waterfront and marina can never be called attractive, but as evening came around it didn't matter to us. We sat outside a restaurant overlooking the Gironde and reminisced about our journey and the journeys the waterway had seen before us. This now immense river has been a route to the vineyards of Bordeaux for more than two thousand years, while for the last eight hundred some of its most common cargoes have been wine destined for the dining tables of England.

That for the past three and a third centuries it has also offered a gateway far beyond Bordeaux to the Mediterranean Sea is the result of an engineering project which, in its time, was of breathtaking scope.

Three hundred and more years ago the technological advances applied to building the Canal du Midi must have been in marked contrast to the pastoral products it carried, but as the world continues to change it throws up even greater contrasts. The Garonne is about to carry a cargo at the opposite end of the industrial spectrum: aeroplanes.

The new Airbus A380 super-jumbo jet is in an advanced state of development in Toulouse, but so large are the components to be delivered there that conventional methods of transportation are inadequate. Having tried to look forward, they've been forced to look back. A compound is being established not far from our restaurant on the Pauillac waterfront where the fuselage, tail and wings of this enormous aeroplane are to be unloaded from ships and transferred by a special pontoon onto a leviathan of a barge – 75 metres long, 14 metres wide and displacing 2,000 tonnes – for transportation up to Landon. Incredibly, from 2004 an entire aircraft will be delivered every week by river in four separate sailings.

That is in the future. For us, our canal trip was now in the past. The next day we unfurled the sails and set off on the morning tide for Royan. *Calypso* was transformed back into a swan, and we were on our way home.

Appendix

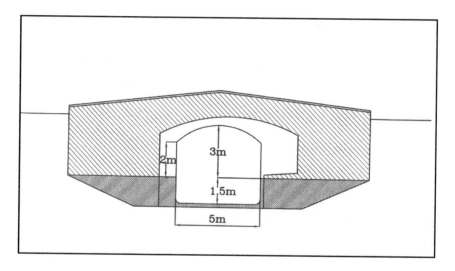

Dimensional constraints

As the oldest of the canals, the Canal du Midi has an official depth of 1.6m and can take barges up to a maximum beam of 5.5m, with an air draft tapering from 2m at each side of the beam up to 3.3m in the centre. If this depth were maintained, it would actually mean that in a line along the centre of the canal the depth would be even greater than 1.6m. In practice (whatever that means), the "working" depth is given as 1.5m, but even this is supposed to apply to wide-beamed, flat-bottomed barges. A keelboat has its maximum depth only over a very narrow width and can therefore take advantage of the likely additional depth in the centre of the channel. The "working" depth for a keelboat could therefore be as much as 1.6m.

The depth can be affected by the water levels which the water table can sustain. In April 2002, for example, the VNF issued a notice warning that extended dry weather had reduced the depth of the Canal du Midi from 1.6m to 1.4m. Difficult as it was to remember that there was *any* dry period during 2002, the exception must have proved the rule. The continuous rain of the late spring and early summer allowed them to restore the levels in June.

Since seawater is denser than fresh water, boats float lower in the canals than at sea. We were told that this would add anything up to 10cms to our draft. In practice, however, we couldn't detect any difference in our waterline – perhaps as a result of the flat-bottomed shape of a modern sailing boat. It might well be different for a motor boat without a keel. The shape of the keel itself can also make a difference. Ours is a "Scheel" keel, with the main weight found in the bulbous casting at the bottom. This makes it more difficult to push through mud. A fin keel on a smaller boat is likely to cut through the muddy bottom more easily. Certainly when the boat was taken out of the water in the UK, the front of the keel had been scoured back to bare metal.

Airdraught depends upon the configuration of a boat, although, unlike barges, most are much higher along the centre line than the sides. In general height underneath the centre of a bridge is around 3.50 metres, although this is reduced to 3.30m on much of the middle section of the Canal du Midi.

The VNF and vignettes

Voies Navigables de France (VNF) is the French equivalent of the British Waterways Board. It operates all the canals in France and its local headquarters for this region are in Toulouse. The addresses of the local offices are:

VNF Toulouse	2 Port St. Etienne, 31079 Toulouse
	Tel: 0561 36 24 24
VMF Carcassonne	Port du Canal, 11000 Carcassonne
	Tel: 0468 71 74 55
VNF Béziers	Pont Rouge, 24500 Béziers
	Tel: 0467 11 81 30

Information is also available on their website: www.vnf.fr/accueil/. Click on "*Transport Fluvial*". Although we received conflicting information, it's still a good idea to check with them first.

A "vignette" (licence) is required for operating a boat on any of the canals and this can be obtained from the VNF offices in Castets-en-Dorthe (entering the canal system from the N), Toulouse, Agde, Narbonne, Arles or Sète (entering from the S). They offer various options, but the most relevant for boats making a transit of the canal is the "holiday" card, valid for a period of sixteen consecutive days. We bought two of them to give us a total of a month.

The *Code Européen des Voies de la Navigation Intérieure* (CEVNI) is required before a vignette can be issued. This is administered in the UK by the RYA and involves learning the rules of the road and the meaning of the various canal signs. A book of the canal signs can also be bought from the RYA. I found it all a rather pointless exercise, firstly because signs on the canal were few and far between, and secondly because if we passed one whose meaning wasn't obvious, I'd completely forgotten what I'd learnt. Since it's obligatory to carry a copy of the rulebook on board, signs can easily be looked up and the most important ones are in the back of the Navicarte guide anyway.

All units in the canals are in kilometres and all the maps are marked in kilometres from the start of the canals – generally in Toulouse. Although the "Point Kilomètre" (PK) is marked on the map, most of the stone markers on the banks have disappeared. According to my calculations there are just under two kilometres in a nautical mile. The speed limit marked as you enter the canal is 5 knots, although elsewhere it's stated as 8 km/hr, which is near enough the same. Any speed above 5 knots starts to leave an unacceptable wash.

Guides and maps

The VNF produce a small "Sailor's Guide" in English, listing all the locks. Information is also available on their website.

A detailed map of the canals is essential. We used the Navicarte edition: Les Voies Navigables du Midi, Éditions Grafocarte. The maps are not north-up and are drawn to a strange scale, greatly enlarging the width. This can be quite confusing at times and it is not easy to locate one's position accurately – the only sure way is to tick off each bridge as it's passed.

The specialist canal maps bear little resemblance to the road maps and, of course, are not available to anyone you might be meeting by road. For this reason the relevant Michelin maps (1cm: 2km) numbered 234 and 235 are also invaluable, and provide a much better idea of the geography of the surrounding countryside.

Other Canal maps:

Guide Vagnon No 7 – Canal du Midi – Les Éditions du Plaisanciers
Guide Fluvial No. 7 – Midi Camargue Aquitaine – Éditions de Breil

Apart from general guides to the region, the Guide du Canal du Midi, Jacques Andre Vert Azur Éditions, provides very detailed information, with comments on each lock (in French).

The website created by a local teacher in Béziers is well worth visiting: www.canalmidi.com. It has quite a comprehensive reading list, although in French. Other sites are:

www.canal-des-2-mers.com
www.canal-du-midi.org
www.lecanaldumidi.com

All the guides work from the north down. Since we went the other way you can always hold this upside down.

Boat hire companies

Connoisseur and Crown Blue Lines are now both now part of First Choice holidays: The Port House, Port Solent, Portsmouth PO6 4TH, telephone: 0870 2408393.

Crown Blue Lines:
Port Cassafières, 34420 Portiragnes   Tel: 04 67 90 91 70
Grand Bassin, 11492 Castelnaudary   Tel: 04 68 94 52 72

Castel Nautique:
BP25, 11150 Bram   Tel: 04 68 76 73 34

Camargue Plaisance:
Port Minervois, 11200 Homps   Tel: 04 68 91 25 99

Connoisseur:
7 Quai d'Alsace, 11100 Narbonne   Tel: 04 68 65 14 55
Palettos Bassos, 11200 Homps   Tel: 04 68 91 24 00
Port de Plaisance, 11800 Trèbes   Tel: 04 68 78 73 75

Locaboat Plaisance:
Port d'Occitaine, 11200 Argens-Minervois   Tel: 04 68 27 03 33

Minervois Cruisers:
38 Chemin des Patiasses, Le Somail 11120 Ginestas
                                                Tel: 04 68 46 28 52
Nautic:
Chemin de la Pageze, 34300 Agde   Tel: 04 67 94 78 93

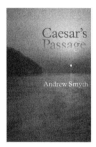

Caesar's Passage, by the same author and short-listed for the Authors' Club Best First Novel Award, is available from all bookshops or through the Gazelle Book Services credit card hotline for the special price of £9.95 plus £2.25 p&p.

Phone: 01524 68765

Wrenched from a carefree childhood on Šipan, a lush and tranquil island in the Adriatic, Milo Beran is plunged into the harshness of life at sea in the 1860s. After jumping ship in Peru, he is thrown into jail in the venal guano port of Callao, where the green shores of his Dalmatian home had never felt so far away.

Described by The Literary Agency as: "*an engrossing read ... fascinating*", this unusual novel is told with real authenticity and will have widespread appeal, particularly to anyone interested in maritime history and the development of 19th century commerce. Essentially a historical thriller, its scenes echo the author's enduring interest in sailing and the sea.

"This book is a ripping yarn with lots of pace. For a book with a racing plot it has some surprisingly poetic descriptions of sea and weather. This is a book which the whole family can share"
Amazon reader's review